THUS FAR ON THE WAY

Fifty Years of Life on the Color Line

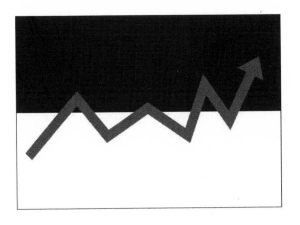

Kathy Grannell Kihanya

Dedication

For my sons,

Dan, Bruce, and Ed

In gratefulness to God

For who they are,

And in gratefulness to them

For what they do.

And for all the joy they have
brought me!

CONTENTS

ACKNOWLEDGMENTS I

AUTHOR'S NOTE II

FORWARD III

PROLOGUE VII

1 FREE, WHITE AND TWENTY-ONE 2

2 WERE YOU SURPRISED? 24

3 ARE THEY YOUR CHILDREN? 41

4 WHAT'S IN A NAME? 58

5 THE RACIAL AND POLITICAL VIOLENCE OF THE 1960'S 64

6 THE WORLD IN BLACK AND WHITE: BUSING IN BOSTON 70

7 MULTICULTURAL EDUCATION 1979-87 87

8 CHEBEAGUE ISLAND 95

9 CHURCH LIFE, 1966-2019 107

10 CURRY COLLEGE   1988-90 123

11 TEACHING IN CATHOLIC SCHOOLS 1990-99 131

12   GED PLUS AT ESAC, 2001-2011   148

13   THE KIHANYA FAMILY IN 2019   164

14   UP 'TIL NOW: THUS FAR ON THE WAY   196

EPILOGUE   216

TIMELINE   223

ABOUT THE AUTHOR   225

ACKNOWLEDGMENTS

Thanks to all who helped me move
thus far along the way.

AUTHOR'S NOTE

The title of this book is borrowed from the third verse of "Lift Every Voice and Sing," better known as the "Black National Anthem" and written by poet and schoolteacher, James Weldon Johnson. That verse, more than any other, speaks to my life's journey, with God as my guide. Lyrics of the entire verse are included here for the reader to consider. Thank you, Mr. Johnson!

Verse 3: *God of our weary years,*
    God of our silent tears,
    Thou who has brought us thus far on the way;
    Thou who has by Thy might led us into the light,
    Keep us forever in the path, we pray.
    Lest our feet stray from the places, our God,
    where we met Thee,
    Lest our hearts, drunk with the wine of the
    world, we forget Thee;
    Shadowed beneath Thy hand,
    May we forever stand,
    True to our God,
    True to our native land

Thus Far On The Way

FORWARD

In these days of white nationalist terrorism and politically correct liberalism, stories all seem to blend together, to have a certain sameness that makes them almost irrelevant. But not all stories. There are stories, individual stories, very personal stories, that can still stir the soul, touch the heart, and change the mind. Kathy Kihanya's story is one of these.

I first met Kathy in the mid-1980s. I was happily serving as an Assistant Dean at Boston University School of Theology, when a friend asked if I wouldn't please agree to serve a tiny United Methodist parish in our neighborhood. Never one to comprehend the concept of overextension, I agreed. I am so grateful I did.

Kathy and David, and their children, were members of that parish, though they had separated by the time I knew them. In a picture still hanging in my study, I am standing proudly with their son Dan, who had just become an Eagle Scout. During the three years I served that little church, we were so busy doing things "in the moment," that I never got to hear the rich story contained in these pages. Oh, I knew some small parts of it. Kathy and I became "spiritual friends," and explored many theological and spiritual concerns. Maybe that is why, when I read her book, nothing shocked me, though I was often astonished by her honesty and transparency. One thing that did *not* surprise me, was the underlying presence of deep love, for her family and friends, and for God.

Even as I write these words, I find myself humbled by Kathy's honesty and faith. Way back in the 80s, I knew her soul was struggling toward something greater, and I think I envied her. Now I cherish her words, her wisdom, and her friendship, knowing that her journey is rich, and it is not finished.

So, I write not as an outsider, but as one who has traveled part of Kathy's journey with her. And, I am better for it.

Laurel Arthur Burton

Lent 2019

O GREAT SPIRIT,
WHO MADE ALL RACES,
LOOK KINDLY UPON THE WHOLE
HUMAN FAMILY,
AND TAKE AWAY THE
ARROGANCE AND HATRED,
WHICH SEPARATE US FROM OUR
BROTHERS AND SISTERS.

– CHEROKEE INDIAN PRAYER

PROLOGUE

My life took a sharp right turn when I met David Kihanya, student, aspiring engineer, Christian, and yes, African (Kenyan). We had so many things in common, yet we were so different. Just like a scene from a romance novel, we met at a college "mixer" as we called it then, at the International House at Tufts University in 1966. Instant attraction across the room, dancing and talking throughout the evening, a walk back to the dorm, and a goodnight kiss that both bolted right through me and terrified me at the same time! After a week of my giving him excuses, I agreed to go out with him, and soon we were together as often as we could be. He wooed me with his stories, his intellect, his hymn-singing, his laughter, his exotic ways, and his obvious attraction to me. We married six months later.

It rained that early autumn day, our wedding day. David said that meant good fortune in his tradition. That the marriage would be "fertile." By contrast, in my tradition it was not a blessing to have rain on your wedding day. I was at the beginning of a very long and arduous journey, one that would take me on an adventure which I was not prepared for, familiar with, or enlightened about, namely inter-racial marriage. For sure it was a path not traveled by many before me, though there have been many since. Unfortunately, there were no GPS's or even maps. I had to find my own way as I went along.

I have been ruminating for twenty-five years about this puzzle: how is it that a white, Protestant, girl from the woods of Maine become the vice principal of a black Catholic school in the big city? It remains incredible to me even now, that I was where I was, and doing what I was doing then, and how I am so very different a person than I was in college even. My life has not been at all what I envisioned as I grew up. And now, being only "thus far on the way," I am still not fully **THERE** yet in my understanding of how race, ethnicity, culture, education, integration, dignity, inclusion and reciprocity should intersect. I pause here, in these pages, to understand where I have been, and how my life has evolved over time. Get ready for a rough ride on the "color line."

Wedding Day, 1966

"The problem of the twentieth century is the color line."

– W.E.B. DuBois, <u>The Souls of Black Folk</u>

ONE – FREE, WHITE AND TWENTY-ONE

Free, white and ten days short of twenty-one, I married a Kenyan-born college student. Not that "free, white and twenty-one" is now, nor ever should have been, in common use. However, it does pretty much describe my life at that time. Being only at the beginning of a lifelong pursuit of racial understanding, I did not know or realize the racist implications of the phrase. White privilege is something that you take for granted – until you are confronted with it. And life has confronted me with it every day of this fifty-three-year journey. My parents taught me to take pride in myself, defend myself and my family, and those like me, and yet do it all with good manners; they were very protective of me and kept a tight leash on my activities right through high school. For instance, I was not allowed to go to movies on Sunday. Unaware, and resting on tradition, they also passed on the essence of white privilege to me, together with the oatmeal and baked beans.

The phrase, "free white and twenty-one" was in common use in the 1960's. I would have considered it a way to brag about my independence, but not as the racist language that I see in it today. In other words, "I can do what I want." I was white, which allowed me to drink from any fountain, swim in any pool and eat at any restaurant as long as I could pay. Sensitivity to such derogatory language had not been part of my education yet. And so the nuances in racism remained undetected. Like, I can say "free, white and twenty-one" if I want to. They say that in the movies, right? And it's about me and not anyone else, right? Everyone says that, right? The ugliness of such phrases would soon have serious implications for my emerging family.

Kathryn Isabel Grannell married David Kariuki Kihanya on September 17, 1966. He was two hours late for the wedding; I was not concerned because I was confident that he was coming and I knew his home-grown penchant for tardiness. David's reason for being late was that he was buying a refrigerator for the apartment. Later on I would lose my patience for his constant lack of punctuality, but not then. The day after the wedding the refrigerator held only a corsage and a half bottle of champagne.

At that time, our marriage would have been illegal in sixteen states, but not in Massachusetts. Then, on June 12, 1967, or nine months later, the U.S. Supreme Court struck down all state anti-miscegenation laws with the case of *Loving vs. Virginia*. It stated: "Under our Constitution, the freedom to marry, or not marry, a person of another race resides with the individual, and cannot be infringed by the State."

While I would prefer to think of myself as a courageous pioneer, the truth is I just wanted to be married to David. It was not some kind of heroic stand for the right to marry whomever I chose. It was not about a civil rights stance but rather about love. Up until then, my life was pretty much controlled by my grandmother's admonition: "Don't make a fuss!" The story of the

Lovings, the plaintiffs in the civil rights case referenced above, seems much like that too, in that they were not out to prove anything except that they loved each other enough to marry. September 17, 1966, was probably the most important day of my life. I was about to have all my ideas about race and racism turned upside down. Life has never been the same again, and that's a good thing. I have been "making a fuss" ever since!

When we come into this world, our only frame of reference is what we knew in the womb – liquid warmth and soothing sounds – and what our senses take in from the immediate environment outside – light blurry objects, stronger sounds, hunger and maybe pain. In the beginning only comfort matters to us; race, gender, sexual orientation, age, size, self-esteem, friendships, religion, language – none of that matters yet. I was blessed with loving parents who guided me gradually into life. Like most, my awareness of the world increased with time and experience. Today, with computers, smart-phones, and constant television, toddlers are exposed to a lot more than I was even at the age of eight or ten. In the nineteen fifties, my parents had more control over my immediate environment, and what I was exposed to, than parents do now. I was naïve. Eventually, however, what my parents could not control was my interest in other cultures, my desire to reach past our mountain valley, and my interest in subjects they did not know much about or maybe did not like.

My hometown, Rumford, is a small paper mill town in western Maine, which at that time was home to about ten thousand residents. It is completely surrounded by mountains. We did not go beyond that valley very often, maybe occasionally to shop. Or to an away high school football or basketball game. The townspeople were 100% white. I left for college at seventeen years old and have never really lived in Rumford since. Nor have any of my twenty-five cousins who were born there. I never saw or met an African American until I was sixteen years old. Mom did buy me an Aunt Jemima doll when I was about eight. And from ten years prior to that, there is an iconic family picture of my grandfather, father, oldest brother and oldest sister on the back porch; Jan is quite obviously holding a black baby doll. My mother referred to black babies as "pickaninnies," a word I have since found was prominent in the film "Birth of a Nation," originally titled "The Clansman" in 1915. Mom used that word only until the Kihanya babies were born and then my brother and sister-in-law adopted two African American babies, and we cautioned her that that was a racial slur.

Recently there was a Facebook post that a black couple lived in Rumford in the 50's and 60's but if so, it was not common knowledge. According to the Rumford Historical Society, William "Napoleon" Thomas arrived in Rumford with Captain Elisha F. Goddard in November 1865. It is reported that the sixteen-year-old former slave, "strayed into the quarters of Company A, of the 12th Maine Regiment while on duty in New Orleans ...and became the Captain's house boy." He returned from the war with the captain, and later on, Napoleon and his son, Clarence, maintained a market garden, selling produce from their farm to neighbors and friends in Rumford (Rumford Historical Society). I never saw them or knew of their existence at the time, and it is obvious from Rumford's Facebook page that most of my peers were unaware of this family as well. It cannot be a mistake that these folks were kept a secret.

My desire to interact with diverse peoples once I got to college likely had its roots in the fact that I did not grow up with many preconceived notions about race. Even the "pickaninny" word was made to seem positive as if the baby was adorable and different. We did not learn in childhood to be afraid of black folks or to dislike them; quite simply, they were not in our collective experience and thus unfortunately outside of our consideration.

My parents were Republican, not because it was in their best interest as blue collar strugglers, but because they had learned that political leaning from their own parents and they never wanted to look beyond that. My father was a union man, a representative for his fellow workers, but he only voted Democrat once and that was really against Barry Goldwater whose very conservative stance was a bit too much for him. I still believe that his political beliefs were at odds with his station in life and with his family's needs. Republican was merely a part of their culture which had been passed down through generations. Many of their convictions were challenged by my marriage and by my brother's adoption of African American children. For the most part, though, we espoused their beliefs about religion, integrity, kindness, the need for education and the need to serve others. Among the five of us children, two grew up to be nurses, one was a preacher, one was a theologian and then me, a teacher. I am proud of that part of my heritage. The generational beliefs about race, ethnicity and culture that we inherited were either disposed of as old-fashioned as we became adults, or more likely we came to dismiss them once we were better educated; as much as we work on these areas, there is always more to work on. My siblings and I do not always agree on these matters either. Still, the culture and beliefs we have passed on to our coming generations are very different from my parents' unexamined prejudices in regard to race, privilege and equality.

From my adult viewpoint now in Boston, it might seem like that cozy world wrapped in the mountains of western Maine might be ideal as a place to grow up, and in many ways, it definitely was. But that town was fraught with some of the very same sociological problems that I have encountered most of my adult life in the city. Prejudice was rampant but the targets were different: Protestants vs. Catholics, Irish vs. French Canadian and WASPs vs. just about any other group in the community. We children heard many, many ethnic slurs against French Canadian, Polish, Jewish and Italian townspeople; that prejudice was definitely not about race, but still it had its roots in people needing to feel superior to someone else. I was always confused about the derogatory slurs, as they seemed to be in conflict with what was being taught in church. I knew instinctively that bigotry was wrong even then.

My childhood memories include the following:

- Wondering why a certain man attended our Methodist Church and yet he was a Democrat. Didn't being Methodist and being Republican go together? I am now a Democrat and the only one of five siblings who remained in the United Methodist Church, so we all found our own way.

- An aunt promised me her pink china teapot if I didn't marry a Frenchman. I fulfilled her wish but never got the teapot!! Ah well, my children are better-looking than the teapot was.

- I recently found a letter I wrote to a friend when I was sixteen. In it I refer to a man as a "typical Jew." I am horrified by those words now.

- One time, I had a friend who scolded me, saying about my then-boyfriend, "But he doesn't look like a Methodist!" I remember asking my-self what a Methodist is supposed to look like. Imagine today if I had to explain how it is that Chiang Kai-shek, Jeff Sessions, Elizabeth Warren, James Comey, and Beyoncé Knowles are all Methodist!

- Crayons were a treasured item in my childhood, and I remember being jealous of someone who had one of those 64-pack boxes of Crayola. In-side that box was one crayon that we referred to as "skin color" or "flesh." Somewhere between white and pink with just a tinge of brown. We were not thinking about any other skin col-ors then. "The Crayola Crayon color name flesh was changed to peach in 1962. Although flesh was included in the original box of 64 Crayola Crayons, we felt it would be insensitive to include it in the commemorative box." (Crayola website)

- There was a family friend who told us, "If you go into a Catholic church, you will lose the power of your legs!"

- We lived next door to a convent where I was forbidden to go. Of course, I did anyway and then stepped in the garden by mistake. The nun told me that she was going to tell the Mother Superior and throughout childhood my nightmares involved a brick-like person with a nun's habit on!

That was the mono-racial, yet biased, framework with which Kathy Grannell came away from her hometown.

I am not just white, but extremely so. Not just by skin color, but white through and through. The ancestry of all four grandparents lies entirely in England, Ireland,

Wales and Scotland. And even then, my Irish forebears were Protestant transplants from England. Three grandparents had immediate forefathers who immigrated to New Brunswick and Prince Edward Island in Canada. And then to Maine. There is a strong line of Protestantism, and Methodism, on both sides of my family, with at least two Methodist ministers in the mix. As Protestants, we were in a minority in Rumford, but that did not stop those in our circle from thinking our ways were RIGHT and all others wrong. White culture was the norm against which all other races and cultures should be measured or so we thought. White is the dominant race in the United States (at least for now), the race with the most advantage. I was born into the advantages of white privilege. I am not comfortable with that thought.

My great-great grandfather went to college. He later became a preacher and a teacher. What advantage did his education give us as a family, as it passed down through the generations? That advantage was certainly not afforded to enslaved African Americans who were not allowed to read and who had their lineage interrupted for over two hundred years. My brother and sister have traced our genealogy extensively and have found that we had five ancestors on the Mayflower and several soldiers in the Revolutionary War and for the North in the Civil War. No extended interruptions in the line. I am very white.

This lineage is not presented just to boast, though it could be perceived as such; on the other hand, I do not want to deny it, nor could I. My ancestors on the Mayflower were invaders to an ancestral Native Indian land here and did not "discover" it. My ancestry is solidly part of who I am. I did not choose the status and yet I was bequeathed white advantages. My ancestry, to me, seems much like the "free white and twenty-one" phrase above: history that does not look as innocent when held up to today's light, and especially to my own adult life experience.

White Anglo-Saxon Protestants (WASP's)

– my forefathers and foremothers – had a history of oppressing others. It was the English, after all, who invaded and colonized Kenya in 1895 and governed it until 1964. Jomo Kenyatta, the first president of a liberated Kenya, said, "When the missionaries came, they taught us how to pray with our eyes closed. When we opened them, they had the land and we had the Bible" (from <u>Facing Mt. Kenya</u>, 1940). David told me that those missionaries were called "pink people" by indigenous Kenyans. The missionaries were British and could well have been in my ancestral line.

I want to doubt that my ancestors ever enslaved others, and yet I find it hard to assess what their attitudes toward race may have been. I do wonder, when I think of the historical contexts in which my family's generations lived, if they were in any way connected to anti-African activity and other types of prejudices. One ancestor sold "spirits" out of Ireland. Could that have been connected to the slave trade? Maybe. Another was a member of the Orange Order in Canada. Given that organization's roots in Great Britain, could there be any anti-Catholic sentiment involved there? Probably. Clues surely, but no proof one way or another.

While being influenced by the cultures of hometown and ancestry, a part of me always questioned those influences, but in those days I would not have dared to say it out loud. In our childhood, Mom read us "Little Black Sambo" and I loved that he was the winner in the end, but I did not know that the stereotypical pictures in the book would become infamous, nor did I know that there are no tigers anywhere in Africa. Still and all, my mother was a good woman who did not have the education and experiences that she worked hard for me to have. And when she became more educated in racial matters, she changed her outlook. She did have a bit of a rebellious streak herself, often choosing to read while delaying housework, and going to work fulltime when most other women did not do that – so that we could go to college.

In my teenage years, I was captivated by the theme and music of "West Side Story" although here too I recognize the stereotyping of urban gang life in my somewhat wiser old age. But those songs, and the Romeo-Juliet romance. Think of Anita singing, "A boy like that will give you sorrow. You'll meet another boy tomorrow. One of your own kind. Stick to your own kind!" I was mesmerized by such themes even then. My sister Beth and I watched and re-watched "Rebel Without a Cause" many, many times and can still recite lines like, "But I am involved. We are all involved!" My best friend in high school was French Canadian. My best friend in college lived in Boston's Chinatown. I was rebellious, inclusive and curious, without being fully aware of it.

As an avid reader from childhood, I loved to roam around the world through books. At church, I was particularly interested in a certain missionary, Dr. Piburn, in Rhodesia, and wanted to go work with him there when I grew up. When I was first in college and the Peace Corps was a new program, I told my parents that I hoped to join after graduation. Dad was upset with me, saying he wasn't working so hard to send me to college just so I could be poor! Sorry Dad, I never did get rich! And yet, my father was also a good man, a hardworking and gentle man who made the wonderful life I have now possible.

The world at large always fascinated me and lured me with possibilities that I had very little access to in Rumford. Several high school teachers tried to give us a taste of what the world was like out there. I was certainly interested in more diversity than was being offered in that mountain-sheltered town. This was the girl who eventually wanted to marry David Kariuki Kihanya.

David grew up very differently than I did. He was born in 1940 in Nakuru, Kenya, the oldest of ten siblings and a member of the Kikuyu tribe. During his childhood, the Mau Mau rebelled against the English and his father was imprisoned for three years during the emergency. As the oldest, he had to help his mother provide for the younger children and thus forego schooling. A bicycle was the only form of transportation and so precious that the children were not allowed to use it. They had no running water and grew much of what they ate. I have never lived in such difficult conditions. After his father's arrival back home, David returned to school and was awarded a scholarship to a private (called public there) Christian high school, and then a sponsorship to Tufts University in the United States when he was twenty-five years old. Nothing in David's background ever made him feel "less-than." In fact, he is a very confident person and encouraged that in his sons. We had in common the twin emphases of education and Christian religion, instilled in us by our parents. What we also had in common was a lack of knowledge about race in America and a great sense of nostalgia and longing for our birth families and home villages. We were both determined to use our intelligence to find a better life. In some ways we each succeeded in that.

Both my son Dan and his wife Molly, and my brother Andy and his wife Dorothy, have traveled to Kenya within the last twenty years. They all went there without David, whose guidance would have been helpful. Dan and Molly waited for a year after their wedding to embark on their honeymoon trip to the land of his ancestors in 1999. I so enjoyed the family stories when they re-turned. They had met their thirty-five Kihanya and Kariuki cousins. They got to see and appreciate both the beautiful scenery and the sites of David's childhood. They had observed all the majestic animals in their native habitat. And they established a strong connection to their Kenyan family that remains today. They were also aware of being regarded as rich Americans with limitless money.

When Andy went to Kenya about fifteen years later, he was not as mesmerized as Dan had been. He and his wife Dorothy were there as participants in a Quaker world-wide conference, but they took the time to seek out David's relatives. Andy found that the

Kenyan and Kikuyu culture, and the practices that he observed were very different from our own. He also found little similarity in how folks treated each other and conducted their daily lives. As an example, one of David's brothers asked Andy, "When is my sister (Kathryn) coming home?" What? How different is that point of view from our vantage point in the United States? To him, even divorced from David, I was still family. We may have never met, and we may not look at all alike, but he claimed me as his sister.

Andy was also able to see firsthand how David had developed the habit of always being late. When David's brother and family invited them to a meal, they had to wait for hours at the table before being served. I could easily identify with the frustration of such a situation from long experience with David. My sons say that it was confusing to them, as children, that their mother thought she was late if she got there at quarter of, and their father thought it was okay to show up two hours late! Cultural differences!

So. "Free" – not so much, now married to a man with his own cultural influences concerning what a wife should be. And penned in by a society that mostly did not agree with my choice of a husband. So. "white" – yes when I was out and about alone with my white advantages, but not when I was out with my family and openly called an "n... lover." So. "Twenty-one" – yes and growing older, abruptly and exponentially. In the course of a thirty-minute marital rite I became bound racially, supposedly tinged by association, and older than my numerical age. Mostly society's choices and not mine. Meanwhile, those white privilege assumptions were still roiling around inside my head. Society, and even friends and family, saw me differently and yet I was still me. Except for the name: Kathy Kihanya I have been ever since. A proud and melodious name. Next to my three sons, the best gift David ever gave me. During our divorce I considered reverting to "Kathy Grannell" but could not bring myself to do so. Besides, Kathy Grannell is a little girl and that name did not and does not properly describe the new woman I had become.

David, Dan and Bruce, 1969

"If you happen to fall in love with someone in another race, it's more difficult, because you have to translate yourself."

— Maya Angelou

TWO – WERE YOU SURPRISED?

At one time I taught in a Catholic elementary school whose student population was maybe twenty percent minority. A few African American students mistrusted the all-white faculty. In some schools, when disciplining students, white teachers have been confronted with "You just don't like me because I'm black." It is a sad commentary on our society that children feel this way and I wonder how much misbehavior is rooted in such feelings. In an attempt to break through one third-grade black student's tough stance, I asked him if he would like to see pictures of my sons. After looking at them, he was very quiet. I asked, "Are you surprised?" Without hesitation, he answered, "No, but were you?" This story still delights me – because of its humor, yes, but also for its honesty and what that young man taught me.

Though never surprised by the physical features of my children, even at birth, I did have difficulty adjusting to the reactions of virtual strangers. Negative reactions to my marriage, my name and my handsome family continue even up to this time, but either these reactions have lessened over time or I have become somewhat inured to them. My way of dealing with the ignorance now is more with humor than with anger, though I can still get pretty steamed up, especially at blatant racism. One comedic instance happened with a woman at a pool about twenty years ago. As my friend introduced me, the new acquaintance asked where my last name came from, a common question when people meet me for the first time. When I replied, "Kenya," she blurted out, "Goodness, you are so very light-skinned!"

A more recent instance that I did not find humorous was when someone referred to my children as "zebra babies" (black and white). They are not animals!! I found this terminology to be very demeaning. I was not brave enough that day to confront the words, as I still have not perfected that art of convincing gently. I try to be as patient as others have been with me in regard to such blunders, but all the same, the ignorance of people who have chosen not to engage with diverse peoples in our society has given me many a good laugh and many a good cry. Ignorance is, by definition, a lack of knowledge. How to gently educate without bursting into laughter or exploding in anger?

White folks are not the only ones to look askance at interracial marriage. I would challenge any white person to stand in an all-black crowd and not be aware of being in the minority. Through experience, I no longer feel isolated at such times. Black folks might feel the same when they are not used to being greatly outnumbered. I remember being invited to a "Sweet Sixteen" party in the black community about 1975 and feeling completely lost, like a "fish out of water." On another occasion, at a public pool and again the only white person there, I asked the woman next to me what time it was, and she literally did not (would not?) give me the time of day, though she had a watch on. Sometimes it is difficult to interpret such an act when no words are spoken, but I would guess it was probably some combination of resentment, lack of experience and also fear that contributed to her silence.

Inter-racial marriage has its detractors certainly, on both sides of the "color line." (credit: W.E.B. DuBois) One time an African-American woman friend explained to me that some black women are offended when white women choose to marry only the most educated and successful black men, leaving black women to choose among those with less potential. When you add to that the unreasonable percentage of black men who are incarcerated, and the hand-me-down circumstance from slavery times of not being allowed to marry, then their own marital possibilities are substantially reduced. They have more than one good reason to be at odds with white women like me.

Most of my knowledge about negative racial interactions came as lessons from those who have experienced it personally and then they had the patience to confront my misconceptions. Time after time, when I have committed social gaffes in the presence of those from a culture or race different from mine, someone has had the patience to pull me aside and correct me, most often with more gentleness than my words or actions deserved. For instance, a friend of Native American heritage taught me the derogatory meaning of "Indian giver" and that the word "Gyp" originated in the debasement of Gypsies. Too bad my ignorance needed such correction, but it did. Black folks must get weary of having to explain these things when they should be obvious in the first place.

I try very hard to listen to those admonitions, take them to heart and not repeat the blunders. At the time of our wedding, my primary concern was not about the reaction of strangers, but rather with that of family and friends. While multiracial marriage had never existed among them before, I believed that most relatives loved me and would maybe be shocked at first, but eventually come around. That is mostly what did happen but not before a series of explosions, negotiations, and then attempts to put the best face on it.

In 1967, the movie "Guess Who's Coming to Dinner?" told of a situation wherein the white daughter of an upper-class family wants to marry a well-educated black man played by Sidney Poitier. While my parents were not as worldly as Spencer Tracey and Katharine Hepburn, the following speech given by Tracey's character delineates some of the concerns those parents had in common with mine. "But you do know – I'm sure you know – what you're up against. There'll be a hundred million people right here in this country who'll be shocked and offended and appalled at the two of you. And the two of you will just have to ride that out. Maybe every day for the rest of your lives. You can try to ignore those people, or you can feel sorry for them and for their prejudices and their bigotry and their blind hatreds and stupid fears. But where necessary, you'll just have to cling tight to each other and say screw all those people! Anybody could make a case, and a hell of a

good case, against your getting married."
Inter-racial marriage was threatening and
unusual to most folks at that time.

My parents were, in fact, terribly shocked
at my impending marriage, not only to a
black man, but also one from a foreign
culture. This was complicated for them by
my pregnancy. They had been aware of my
dating David, but in a cowardly and
regrettable act, I had lied and told them I
would break up with him, with no intention
of doing so. They probably had no idea
exactly where Kenya was, other than
somewhere in Africa. They would have had
to check a map. My mother was sure I would
contract syphilis; that misconception was
particularly painful though her lack of
knowledge was understandable. She
wanted me to go live in an unwed mothers'
home and give up the baby. Ironically, I
worked with that very same home 40 years
later, helping the residents there attain their
GED's.

In a series of meetings over the course of a

particular weekend, we negotiated all the most immediate decisions. There were strong emotions on all sides, but sometimes my sense of detachment made it feel like they must be talking about some other person. I was focused on marrying David before the next semester started, but my own free will seemed to have deserted me. David brought a Kenyan friend with him to these meetings and probably should have had further support of his own. He asked me if he needed an attorney (no). Mom and Dad tried to convince me that it would be a very difficult life; in the end, they were correct in that, but I was not really considering their words. I was fancifully dreaming that David and I would dance off into a future of lovingkindness and picket fences, maybe in the majestic highlands of Kenya! Reality was only allowed in when it was absolutely necessary. The pregnancy was such a reality.

My brother-in-law, Jim, served as mediator for the negotiations and had to intervene often. My sister Jan made all the arrangements for the wedding, including the venue, the flowers, and even champagne for our first night as a married couple. Without her, we would probably have resorted to a Justice of the Peace near the college. I vividly remember the emotional pain of letting my parents down, and feeling like no matter what, that disappointment would never go away. I cared deeply about their feelings. They had had such high hopes for me and none of those hopes had included the present situation. They bought me a wedding dress and attended the wedding, trying to smile. Their pain had a profound effect on me but I toughed it out, and ran through, over and around it. Somehow, I survived the battle; I had no idea how much more conflict there was to come. This part of my life's journey not only had twists and turns in it, but also some traffic snarls that would look like knots on any map. No straight stretches at all.

Eventually, after getting to know and love David and their grandbabies, my parents' disappointment and disbelief did ease into the background. They were very proud of all fifteen of their grandchildren and mine were no exception. Our sons were equally included in the family pictures on their walls and tables. Grammie and Grampy never missed celebrating all their birthdays. When Dan became an Eagle Scout at eighteen, they attended the celebration and then placed a bragging article about it in their local newspaper. Our sons were fully included, and loved as family, as was David.

My four siblings, and their spouses and children, have been loving and supportive of my lifestyle from the beginning. My sister, Jan, hosted our wedding reception while her husband, Jim, an Episcopalian priest, conducted the ceremony. Later on, they took care of Dan while I finished up my college courses. My oldest brother, Dick, lived with us for a short time and brought newborn Bruce home from the hospital in his car. After my brother Andy and my sister-in-law Dorothy adopted an African American boy and girl, Kyle and Susan, we often compared notes on our children, how they interacted with their peers and how we were forging a path for future bi-racial and multi-racial families. My youngest sister, Beth, was the only one not yet married in 1966 and, as a pediatric nurse and a sister, she delighted in my babies. After her marriage, she and Jack welcomed us to their new Florida home as we celebrated our first big vacation as a family in 1978.

Several relatives never spoke to me again, and one in particular would not even acknowledge my presence in a room. Another said mean and despicable things about Beth and me, in our presence. Sometimes the ones I expected disdain from would surprise me with gifts and love and kindness in abundance. Others would speak to me as if I did not have a family, never asking about the boys or how David was – as if ignoring my marriage and children would make them disappear. I was proud of my family and wanted a chance to tell how wonderful they were. Always the most painful repudiations were the ones that were left unsaid, but still obvious. Painful too were and are the times when white strangers assume when I am out alone that I will agree with their racist ideas and I have to set them straight.

One relative decided AFTER my marriage that I needed to know the biblical basis for not marrying someone of a different race. This came in the form of an invitation for David and I to watch a video which I thought at the time would be about being a better Christian or something like that. What it turned out to be was a listing of bible verses that purportedly show that God does not want us to intermarry, mostly from the Old Testament. Verses such as: "Furthermore, you shall not intermarry with them; you shall not give your daughters to their sons, nor shall you take their daughters for your sons." (Deuteronomy 7:3) It is said that "Birds of a feather flock together," but that is not biblical but rather an English proverb that originated in the sixteenth century. The Bible does warn Christians in the New Testament not to intermarry with unbelievers, but this was not about race or culture, but rather about Christians not marrying with other religions. Those verses were like this: "Do not be unequally yoked together with unbelievers. For what fellowship has righteousness with lawlessness? And what communion has light with darkness?" (2 Corinthians 6:14 NKJV) David and I had Christianity in common, and those verses did not seem to apply in any way. And, of course, the video totally overlooked the verse from Isaiah 11:6 which says: "The wolf will live with the lamb, the leopard will lie down with the goat, the calf and the lion and the yearling together; and a little child will lead them." Not wanting to cause a scene (Don't make a fuss!), I watched the video until the end, said nothing, and walked away. David and I had a long discussion about the video later, in which we uncharacteristically agreed about its foolishness. As my mother taught me, "The devil can quote scripture for his own purposes." (William Shakespeare, <u>Merchant of Venice</u>)

Some of the stories I have presented here seem funny because of how ridiculous they are, on first hearing, but there is a whole ice-berg of ignorance and hostility beneath them. These situations have phased out in my family, as did the generation that held them; I need to acknowledge that that generation had no training, no real knowledge or understanding of the world beyond their own. In my parents' generation the biggest problem with a marriage had been when my Protestant aunt married a Catholic! In my own generation, the surviving nineteen cousins, are all in contact with me now and show me respect and love; I love them too! All of us moved away from Rumford a long time ago, and live in much more metropolitan places, full of diversity, and full of the people and tools that help all of us to understand each other better. Thus, our extended family now includes members originally from Egypt, India, China, Cape Verde, and Trinidad.

Six or seven of David's extended family now live in the United States or have studied here. I have only met one of my nephews from Kenya; he is a United States resident now. He too is named David (Kamau), within the Kikuyu naming tradition of David Kihanya, as his mother's oldest brother. I have also met one of David's second cousins, Wambui Kihanya, and she is delightful! Actually, she and my daughter-in-law Molly both worked at Microsoft in Seattle and co-workers have been known to wonder how Molly and Wambui could be related! Sometimes this stuff is fun!

In the course of about eighteen months in 1966 and 1967, my life underwent a near complete revision. I got married. I had two extremely difficult childbirths. I graduated from college. David applied for permanent residence in the United States and I was grilled over and over about whether I had only married him to give him a chance for citizenship. At that time, I was pregnant with our second child, Bruce, and was very tempted to ask if they thought I would carry it so far as to bear two children? Reality had abruptly wiped out all the fanciful dreams of picket fences. We were extremely poor, living on $60 a week. David wanted me to apply for welfare; when I refused, he went to work fulltime, trying to study evenings. We waded through it all, but it took a toll on our marriage which never really recovered. Most likely any marriage with that amount of agitation and disruption in the beginning could not survive, never mind the added discrimination and dispiriting isolation from society that our inter-racial marriage had brought. We did not prepare, and we were not ready.

From the outset I knew that a difference of skin color is not a problem and still believe that. However, a cultural difference between spouses **IS** a big problem. Still, I would never advise a young multi-racial couple not to marry. Instead I would advise them to make sure they know each other very well first, and that they should research each other's cultures and families and talk about the differences. Despite my own experience, I still support multi-racial marriage as a concept, but it does not automatically work in all realities. My advice: you better be strong and love each completely, culture, race, hopes, dreams, marital roles and all!!

Bruce, Ed, Dan, 1973

Rejoice and shout with laughter
Throw all your burdens down
If God has been so gracious
As to make you black or brown.
For you are a great nation,
A people of great birth
For where would spring the flowers
If God took away the earth?
Rejoice and shout with laughter
Throw all your burdens down
Yours is a glorious heritage
If you are black, or brown.

— Gladys Casely-Hayford, Sierra Leone

THREE – ARE THEY YOUR CHILDREN?

My babies were adorable, full of personality and inordinately smart! We named them according to Kikuyu tradition. Our first son, Daniel, is named after his paternal grandfather, Kariuki, and holds that as his middle name. Bruce was named after his maternal grandfather, my Dad, and holds my maiden name Grannell as his middle name. Edward was named after David's oldest brother and holds the middle name of Muruthi (Lion). And yes, those middle names did get used when they were kids and in trouble. They all walked by 10 months of age and Dan and Bruce were speaking in full sentences at one year.

One day when Dan and Bruce were probably one and two years old, I took them to the local grocery store in their double stroller. As we entered the store, we came upon two girls about eight and ten years old, both white. They remarked on how cute the boys were, then asked, "Are these your children?" I said yes and then, as they were walking away, I heard one of them say, "I didn't know that!" Yes, brown babies can be birthed by Caucasian mothers. I would have loved to hear the family discussion when they got home. Or maybe not. In any case, they would not be as surprised by a bi-racial child in 2019, with all the exposure to diversity young people now have in classrooms, in the media and on social forums.

Two things that have not changed for we Kihanyas over the years is people thinking it is alright to ask where our name is from, and "What are you?" Well, human, male or female, Christian, extrovert, human really. Society seems to need to classify others in terms of race, culture and country of origin. In answering these two questions, we are placed in the position of having to explain more than we may want to, and to answer about personal information. Why do others need that information? Often in order to form a judgment, positive or negative. It would be fine with me if these questions came further on in a friendship, but why do utter strangers think it is okay to ask such personal questions?

A third thing that has caused problems for us from time to time began as soon as we were married. When David and I started to look for an apartment to rent near the college, we encountered landlords who suddenly had "already rented" or who would "have to get back to you." And there was even one who insisted that he had to see our marriage license before he would consider renting to us. In the end we found a perfect place on the next street to the college, with a very considerate and accommodating landlord.

It is not easy figuring out where you want to live as a multiracial family, and we decided to try Boston, but it took three neighborhood moves for us to all feel comfortable. As our family size increased, and we were no longer students at Tufts, we moved on first to Brighton, thinking that at least the students in the area would be more open to us. They were, but the old guard was not. So, then we moved on to Mattapan where we found a different set of problems. Boston is infamous for having distinctly homogeneous neighborhood enclaves – at that time – not so much now. The North End for Italians, Southie and West Roxbury for Irish, Roxbury for Blacks, Mattapan for Jewish people, Jamaica Plain for Latinos, etc. So, we moved to Mattapan in 1969, and when we arrived, David was the only person of color on a predominantly white Jewish street. There was a lot of redlining in Boston at that time, and by the time we moved away eighteen months later, I was the only white person on the street. Total change in population in just that short time. Fortunately, in 1971, we found a new housing development in Hyde Park through family connections, and that is where the boys spent the next twenty-three years, all the way through college.

Our sons' skin tones are all similar, somewhere in the middle ground of my extremely pale and David's much darker skin. African American folks often refer to them as "light-skinned." It did surprise me that my children were still susceptible to sunburn. My niece Diane has a mixed-race family, too, with three sons whose skin tone is much like my own sons. She told me that when people remark about how little her sons look like her, she replies, "They look like me on the inside." Me too! My sons look very much like each other, to the point that people often mistake Bruce for Ed, and vice versa, even referring to them as twins. They do not resemble my birth family and David has never said that they look like anyone in particular in his. Bruce has some Grannell physical features and Ed is like my father in ways that I have never been able to name outright. They are themselves!

Dan, Bruce and Ed grew up in a much different world than either of their parents had. We had hoped that the racial climate might improve over time, but the infamous Boston school busing crisis started in 1974 when they were seven, six and two years old. (See Chapter 5). Much of the animosity caused by the court order, which I agreed with, was overheard by, and taught to children, as parents, politicians and their peers gave opinions about the situation, including racial slurs. I did my best to counter that venom by participating in the school parent council, keeping informed and asking neighbors and friends their opinions about events. One day, as Dan and I were walking down the street, a neighborhood child called Dan a "n...." Right in front of me! My children will still tell you that I can over-react (is that possible?) to racist put-downs, and I was about to do just that when Dan placed his 10 year old arm in front of me, looked squarely in the eyes of the offender and said, "What is YOUR problem?" All the air went out of the child. When he did not get the exasperated and outraged reaction he expected, he seemed flummoxed and ran off. That was one of many, many times when my children knew better than I what to do, simply because they lived it every minute, and I did not. They even had to advise me about where they could not go after dark.

Ironically, my over-reactions seem to have

come from my habits of whiteness. Nobody should try to debase me or mine!! Another example of such overreaction was a day in maybe 1977. One of my son's schoolmates was hanging around with us at the local laundromat where I was doing the laundry. It happened to be the day of one of the first observances of Martin Luther King Day in Massachusetts, and I sat talking to my children about what the holiday signified. The schoolmate interrupted us, saying, "My father says that we shouldn't have a Martin Luther King Day because he started all the trouble." In other words, Boston's busing trouble. Unfortunately, again I did not take the time to exploit this teachable moment and instead retorted, "Your father is stupid." Not one of my best moments. I was angry and defensive. The youngster told me that he was going to tell his father on me, and I replied, "Go ahead. He won't be surprised by who said it!" Probably did not improve race relations and may have even set it back a bit with my childishness. The only positive in there is the possibility that my own children realized precisely how important MLK was to me and to the country. There is every chance that I embarrassed them too. I never did hear from the boy's father. Just as well.

Our children had extensive access to what society perceived as their heritage. Their parents were a New Englander and a Kenyan; those are the cultures they should have had the most access to and did. However, in the world at large, and particularly in their day-to-day activities, they were and are considered African American (or Afro-American as we said in those days). Bi-racial children have no voice in how they want to be identified. It was white folks who decided who is white and who is not. The "one-drop" rule was initiated in the nineteenth century, stating that all people of mixed race in the United States should be automatically identified only as black. This same system does not apply to those of other races, Asian or Native American for instance. If we look back at the 1920 census in the United States, there was a classification for mulatto, a word that means having one white and one black parent. After that census the "mulatto" category was eliminated and the "one drop" rule was reinstated meaning that if you were even a little bit so, you were/are black.

It was not convenient for white masters in the south to claim the children they shared with their enslaved workers as their own or part white. They could pretend that they were not theirs, just by saying they were black like the rest of their victimized laborers. During slavery, and from that time forward, African Americans have referred to children of mixed ancestry as "high yellow," especially when they are very light-skinned.

Our sons got to celebrate their New England heritage each summer in Maine, with cousins. However, their only connection to Kenyan and African culture was their Dad and a few of his friends. Being Kenyan-American was not something they had in common with anyone else. They watched the Boston Marathon every year when Kenyans almost always came in first. They did not get to publicly celebrate their Kenyan heritage until Barack Obama became President. And how we all celebrated then! President Obama is six years older than Dan. Someone once asked me why it is that President Obama never claimed his white heritage. Well, he certainly did not deny it in his books or in his presidency. He told stories of his mother and his grandparents; yes, but how would it have played out if he claimed to be white? Society has dictated that he is black. Everyone wants to belong and even until this day, bi-racial (black/white) folks are classified as black, a place they are more welcome and comfortable.

My sons and I were exposed to any children's book I found at the library or bookstore dealing with black history and culture, and any film depicting black heroes or the evolution of civil rights. Their parents had not experienced these kinds of stories, but we made sure they were aware of the culture that they were living in right then. We prayed together every night asking blessings for their grandparents in Maine as well as their *Shosho* and *Nguka* in Kenya. We completed the ritual by singing, "Morethe Wakwa"– a Kikuyu rendition of the Twenty-third Psalm.

Unfortunately, sometimes it was outsiders who taught our sons the negative part of their heritage – in the form of prejudice against them. A blatantly racist incident that we had as a family took place in traffic about 1979. The five of us were in our car, on the way north to Maine. I was not feeling well and sat in the back seat with the boys, a pillow under my head. A state police officer passed us on the left, staring fixedly into the car. David was not speeding or driving erratically. The car had a valid inspection sticker and registration. We were just a family out on a ride, albeit an unusual family then. After passing us, the police officer slowed down, then doubled back to pass us again, this time on the right. Then he slowed a second time, let us pass and turned on his siren for David to pull over. As he approached the car, he addressed me first, instead of David, asking if I was alright. Obviously, he thought that a white woman resting in the back of a black driver's car might be in some danger. He may have had some tact or sensitivity training to at least pretend it was a legitimate stop, and so he then asked David for his license and registration. We went on our way. We had done nothing wrong. Still it was unnerving. This incident is one of the instances that that necessitated "the talk" with our sons when they got their licenses.

Another such story happened about ten years later when Dan was eighteen and had just become an Eagle Scout. A body was found in the woods about a mile from our house. On my way to pick up the boys at Scouts that same night, I had to travel the somewhat remote road near where the death had taken place (unbeknownst to me at the time). As I drove along, I encountered a group of about ten teenagers milling about and yelling in the middle of the road. They stepped aside and let me pass. The next day when I heard about the dead body, I decided that it might help the police to know about the group that had been in the road, even though I had not recognized any among them. I decided to visit the local police station with my information, but Dan begged me not to go, saying, "Mom this is not the city of brotherly love." When I insisted, he said he would go with me for support. When we got to the station and sat down, I began my story but suddenly noticed that there were two policemen behind us craning their necks this way and that, as they stared at us from behind and seemed to be taking particular note of Dan. When I asked why they were doing that, they replied that they were just there to assist. Afterwards I had to admit that Dan had been right to warn me. It's strange that I do not remember if they ever caught the killer, but I do remember warning myself to think twice before I volunteered to be a witness again. And people wonder why folks refuse to come forward as witnesses lest they become "persons of interest" themselves.

Throughout their childhoods, our sons attended cultural events in Boston with us — "Black Nativity" at Christmastime, Chinese

New Year parade in February, the Fourth of July concert on the Esplanade, the fall Jazz festival in the South End, and Italian Saints Festivals in the North End. Of course, they already knew about music and sports stars who were African American; nearly every child knew about and embraced those folks, but they were not necessarily the models that I wanted them to emulate. I wanted to ensure that they knew historical black heroes as well: Mary McLeod Bethune, Rosa Parks, Crispus Attucks (a Bostonian!), Frederick Douglass, Thurgood Marshall, Harriet Tubman.

As a mother, as a white mother used to privilege, I was determined that my children would have any and all advantages that any child around us had. Their elementary school was in walking distance from our apartment and was a magnet school with a theme of multicultural education. All three were excellent students and seemingly well-regarded by the teaching staff and principal. All three delivered the newspaper in the neighborhood and were treated well by their customers.

One year I took them to see Santa Claus at Jordan Marsh and chose the line for the black Santa (it *was* shorter!). When we got to the front, Dan said, "That's not Santa!" Unfortunately, our <u>A Visit from St. Nicholas</u> book at home depicted a Santa who was definitely white.

Each of the boys was active first in Cub Scouts and then in Boy Scouts. Here was another structured activity where they would be safe. In 1985, Bruce and Ed had the opportunity to go to an international jamboree in Ireland. They have grand memories of that experience, in a place beyond our shores, meeting people from all over the world. An experience they would not have had otherwise, especially at that age. Ed, Bruce and Dan all earned their Eagle Scout badges, accomplishments of which I am still very, very proud, as are they.

A difficulty for all three of them was having to constantly explain our "different" family. And later on, that was exacerbated by their parents' separation and eventual divorce. How to explain why it is that they are brown when their brown father was not around all the time? Yes, I did teach them that they were brown (they were! /are!) but a kind and patient African American neighbor convinced me that that was not in their best interest, and I changed the designation to Afro-American. In addition to all this, Ed was struggling with what we thought at the time was learning disabilities and what we now know to be Asperger's Syndrome.

One example of how we often brought in laughter to lighten the mood occurred about 1980. We were out at a buffet restaurant for Mother's Day. There was a sign posted: "Free dessert for mothers." The boys were far ahead of me in the line but since they could not take their trays to the table before the bill was paid, Dan doubled back just as I was asking about the free dessert. With a straight face he said to the server, "Is she trying to say she's my mother?" Dan has a great sense of humor, but he went a bit too far that day! That poor waitress got so flustered, and I admonished him for being a wise guy. Still, I think it's funny now. You might as well laugh.

David and Family, Nairobi Airport, 1965

"What's in a name? That which we call a rose by any other word would smell as sweet"
– <u>Romeo and Juliet</u>, William Shakespeare

FOUR – WHAT'S IN A NAME?

Names change all the time. Eritrea used to be Ethiopia. Beijing used to be Peking. My mother decided it was more stylish to call herself Edna Mae rather than the Edna May we found on her Social Security account in her later years. My daughter-in-law legally changed her name to Molly when she was only sixteen. My grandmother disliked her name, Isabella, and was known as Bella throughout adulthood. When my parents decided that my middle name would be in her honor, she would not allow the original, so my middle name is Isabel, not really a namesake. My maiden name, Grannell, was pronounced in rhyme with flannel until World War II, when the five remaining Grannell adult males decided to pronounce our name as Grannell, rhyming with bell, because that was more in line with the spelling and thus easier to pronounce. There are still folks, even seventy-five years later, who insist that we are pronouncing it wrong. We should all get to name ourselves, as individuals, as families, as racial groups and even as nations; no one else can or should. It is a courtesy that should be extended to anyone because we all want to maintain our own dignity. I know who I am better than anyone.

I learned early in life to be precise with personal names because my mother was an identical twin and despised being called "Twinny" as a child – as if she was not a separate person with her own identity. A name is simply a shortcut that allows us to refer to someone without having to use a long list of identifiers. I can refer to my son as "Ed" instead of having to say, "You know, that tallish handsome fellow with light brown skin who always wears that Patriots jacket." Even when referring to a group of people, it is easier to say "black" or "white" but this is often where we run into trouble. A racial or ethnic slur is a shortcut too, only it is teeming with hatred, ignorance, debasement and condescension.

Not unlike my mother, groups want to claim their own identity and not acquiesce to the names that others want to tell you that you are. Naming a group becomes a label over time. So, society as a whole has developed the habit of placing folks in either the white or black category, but this really leaves my children and grandchildren with no choice but to follow society's dictates that they should be identified as black.

There has been much discussion about African Americans changing how they want to be named over the last one hundred years. First "colored," then "Negro," then "Afro-American," then "Black" and late years, "African-American." Of course, such an evolution would be necessary, as pride and self-respect grew during this one-hundred-and-fifty-year history of African Americans having to reconstruct their histories from very little written material, and having to regenerate their oral traditions into written form. All because of the slavery that they did not choose. Like Edna, Molly, Isabella and the Grannells above, black folks want to have control over perceptions of who they are. The second principal of

Kwanzaa is: "To define ourselves, name ourselves, create for ourselves, and speak for ourselves, instead of being named and spoken for by others." While some folks have been confused by the progression of these racial identifiers, those others should not have any choice of how the names change or how often.

So, while one might ask why my sons are not commonly named as white/black or bi-racial, it is history and society that dictates the answer. Research shows that among African Americans in the United States, twenty-four percent have DNA from European backgrounds. (Henry Louis Gates, In Search of our Roots: How 19 Extraordinary African Americans Reclaimed their Pasts.) Beginning in slavery, the masters bedded and raped enslaved women and the offspring were not claimed by those white fathers. Can you imagine Sally Hemmings trying to say her children were white because Thomas Jefferson was white? What would have happened to her? This tradition of bi-racial and multi-racial persons being designated exclusively as black-only over many generations continues until now. But a time is coming when we will need better descriptors of a person's racial/biographical inheritance – or due to the complexity we dispense with categories altogether. Amen.

"Violence is as American as apple pie."
— H. Rap Brown

FIVE – THE RACIAL AND POLITICAL VIOLENCE OF THE 1960's

Both President Kennedy and Malcolm X were assassinated in the mid-1960's, in my college years and before I met David. Like so many, I can remember exactly where I was on campus when I heard the news of the President's death. Students were weeping and screaming all around me. The chapel bell was ringing incessantly. Classes were cancelled that Friday and into the following week. We all felt a profound sadness. I had not entirely formed my own political opinions yet, and my parents had not voted for Kennedy. However, this assassination did not seem as much like a political act as an attack on our country, and it shook me emotionally.

As already noted, I arrived at college my freshman year with no experience interacting with people of other races. In a naïve and idealistic way, I was unsure of how to approach such situations. Therefore, I went out of my way to smile every time I passed a black student. In my ignorance, how foolish that must have looked. In my defense, it was well-intended even if ridiculous. At least they probably had a good laugh at my expense.

This lack of knowledge, and failure to pursue it at that time, gave me a very negative view of Malcolm X. It appeared, on the surface at least, that he hated all white people and many white folks would have agreed with that. I see how wrong that was, with more reading and exploring about his life, philosophy and religion. Within my still-childish framework, I did not react at all when he was killed in 1965. I was much more interested in Martin Luther King and his peacefully resistant Civil Rights Campaign. That was a style I could identify with. And Dr. Martin Luther King was a minister, another factor that I identified with.

As with JFK's death, I also remember my exact location when I heard that Martin Luther King had been shot to death in Memphis, in April 1968. David's radio alarm mournfully announced the news the next morning. I was distraught and ranting about the injustice of it all. It wasn't fair that a man of peace died in violence, or that his young wife and children would have to go on without him. Or that he could no longer lead the nation into a more just society. I cried out, "Why did it have to be him? Why couldn't it have been H. Rap Brown?" H. Rap Brown, as a leader of SNCC and then the Black Panthers, had been advocating violence, as opposed to King's peaceful ways. David was taken aback, and then angry, at my outburst. He asked me, "Why did it have to be either of them? Why did it have to be a black man?" He was right of course. Why indeed?

The words of Robert F. Kennedy to a mostly black crowd, on the occasion of Dr. King's assassination were pretty much what I was feeling at the time: ""For those of you who are black and are tempted to ... be filled with hatred and mistrust of the injustice of such an act, against all white people, I would only say that I can also feel in my own heart the same kind of feeling." A definite difference was that I had no personal or family experience in losing someone in that way, as Robert Kennedy had. That murder was so, so violent and so, so heart-wrenching for anyone who cared about race relations and civil rights at the time.

David's frankness after my outburst was once again an example of how it is that most of what I know now about racism came from situations like this – when someone was willing to confront my racism and my white advantage. It is not enough to admire and support only those black folks who conform to white ideas of comportment and philosophy. All of us must give due consideration to all individuals within a culture and listen to all challenges to our protected status as whites. We must work at understanding what the backgrounds and histories are that have produced the thinking of the oppressed. We all need to have a desire and a willingness, to adjust our own opinions in order to understand and support them.

The assassination of Robert Kennedy that same June made it seem as if assassinations were becoming a way of life in our nation. David often spoke of the pervasive violence as something he would not have believed before he came here. It seemed as if every time we found a leader who could give us hope for a better world, he or she was gunned down; then it felt instead like the world was worse. College campuses were in upheaval over the Vietnam War, racism, politics and all types of injustice. Students were angry and ready to take matters in their own hands. They were not entirely wrong, but their parents believed they were. How was any of this making things better? What kind of world had I brought children into? And then things got even worse for us, specifically about race; residents of Boston began an all-out race war.

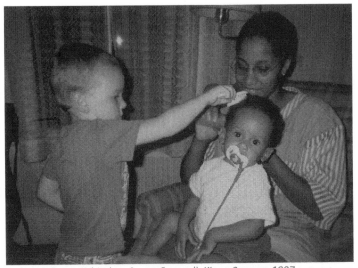

Jimmy Whitaker, Susan Grannell, Kiana Sawyer, 1997

"When elephants fight, it is the grass that suffers."

— Kenyan Proverb

SIX – THE WORLD IN BLACK AND WHITE: BUSING IN BOSTON

The 1974 court order from Judge Garrity required Boston Public Schools to comply with the state law called the "Racial Imbalance Act." That act made it mandatory for all school districts in the state to treat students in all racial categories equally when it came to educational access. Local school districts were to take measures to ensure this equality. The Boston School Committee, in an NAACP lawsuit, *Morgan vs. Hennigan* (February 1973), was accused of deliberate discriminatory practices against black students. Judge Garrity agreed, and thus began the busing crisis in Boston. A desegregation plan was ordered to be in place before the 1974-75 school year began. The city was split apart by those on one side agreeing with the order, and those who disagreed, and did not want their children bused out of their own neighborhoods. They were willing to organize and protest against it. Those in agreement with the order were mostly black and those opposed, mostly white. It was an embarrassing time to be a Bostonian and it has taken a long time for the city to recoup its reputation nationally.

One of the requirements under the court order was that all families would have to complete a form designating what race their child was. To the best of my recollection, there were seven choices: Black, White, Hispanic Black, Hispanic White, Asian-American and Pacific Islander, Native American, and "Other." Later in the process the "Other" category was broken down still further, ending in "Other, Other." Many of us played with the classifications to get the assignment school we most desired. For instance, some checked off Native American, justifying it by reasoning, "My child was born here." To my knowledge, no parent's designation was ever questioned. Prior to busing, when Dan was about to start kindergarten, we wanted him to go to an inner-city school with a predominantly black population and an excellent academic reputation. We were advised that we could get him admitted if we designated him as white; I am not proud of doing that, but we moved to a new neighborhood before the school year began anyway. By the time of the busing order we were at a loss to know how to designate our bi-racial children according to the categories presented, so we checked off "Black." The next year we switched it to "Other." By the time that all three were in school, we were checking off "Other, Other." That is what they were, within the limited guidelines afforded us, but inaccurate all the same. The school department may have needed those designations to implement the judge's order but why couldn't they be all of who they were (are)? Again, no school authority ever questioned our choices.

The Ohrenberger School opened in our neighborhood in 1972 and served as the neighborhood elementary school for the two years before busing. In September 1972, Bruce was in Kindergarten I (4-year olds), Dan was in Kindergarten II (5-year olds) and Ed was two weeks old. When the busing order was implemented in 1974, the student population at the Ohrenberger was about 500, almost evenly divided between black and white children. Under the order, the Ohrenberger became a "Magnet School," meaning that students from all over the city were eligible to attend, even if they had to be bused there. It was a very popular choice for parents throughout the city. This meant that some neighborhood children (mostly white) would be assigned elsewhere, while children of color from other neighborhoods would have full access to the school, so that it could comply with the Racial Imbalance Act. Being "Other, Other," ensured that my children would easily be accepted. It also meant that their parents had to have an evolving sense of race markers. They all stayed there through Grade 5.

The court order required that each school have a Racial Ethnic Parent Council (REPC) that would monitor the school's programming and identify any activity not in compliance with the court order. Participating in that council, I found it a bit difficult to choose whether I was representing white parents or black children. Again it required a choice for me and I chose to be a white parent which also skewed the balance a bit since I would tend to favor what was best for my black child. Being on that council was an intense and thought-provoking experience. I have vivid memories of the empowered and fair-minded parents I worked with there. They were ardent supporters of the court order for the most part and took the work we were doing seriously. They were also open to change and to being inclusionary, which takes much more energy and yet is so rewarding.

The Commonwealth of Massachusetts, under the Racial Imbalance Act, designated funds to assist the Boston Public Schools in implementing the court order. These funds were known as Chapter 636. Most of that money was used to pair individual schools with local colleges and to build programming that facilitated the desegregation process. The Ohrenberger, as a "Magnet School," was given a magnet theme of "Multicultural Education." The local college we were paired with was Emmanuel College in the Back Bay. The Parent Council was assigned to assist and support the development of the magnet theme.

While helping to develop the Multicultural Education program, the Parent Council worked with teachers to include all 44 cultures and ethnicities represented in the school, their customs and holidays, and their differences and similarities. A task force of three parents, three teachers and a consultant from Emmanuel produced an outline of the proposed curriculum programming and a budget ($58,000), which then went to the Parent Council for approval at its next meeting.

Part of the design of the Parent Council was that a teacher was chosen to coordinate the meetings and serve as secretary to document actions taken. This position meant that the parents had no privacy or autonomy in their decision-making, though we did not realize it at the time, and were not concerned about it initially. In the spring of 1978, our secretary, unbeknownst to council members, advertised our next meeting as a chance for other parents to give input on the use of Chapter 636 funding. That by itself would not have been a problem, but he did not tell us. We had expected the meeting to include council members, the secretary, and maybe a few other interested parents. We arrived to a meeting room that had been moved to the library because of the extraordinary size of the crowd. The chairs for the council itself were set up front and center, facing the crowd. Participants were mostly white and demanded that the Chapter 636 money be spent on a new gym teacher. There were many in the crowd that I did not recognize as parents. Later we learned that some were there to represent R.O.A.R. (Restore Our Alienated Rights), an anti-busing group which was often in the newspaper for activities in opposition to the Judge Garrity order. It was difficult for the council to maintain order. The people were rowdy, loud and insistent. We were blind-sided and unprepared for the situation.

One particularly outspoken woman stated, "We don't need multicultural education for our children. We can teach them that at home. We can take them to the Chinese New Year parade outside of school time. What we need is a gym program during the school day." Later, when we had more time to consider her remarks, we realized that we should have answered, "We don't need a gym program. We can take them to Red Sox games. We need a multicultural program to help these newly-integrated students to understand each other better." Ah well, that irony would probably have been lost on the protesters. In the end, we really had no choice anyway. The funds *had* to be spent on easing the process of desegregation and not on providing services that the school system itself should have been providing anyway, like gym. The Boston Public Schools had built a beautiful new school, with a fully equipped gym, and then did not provide a gym teacher. The protesting participants in the meeting were correct in that assessment!

The Racial Ethnic Parent Council sent the secretary/teacher a letter dismissing him from the position because of his actions. After his appeal, he was allowed back in the position because of court guidelines stating that the principal had the right to assign a teacher of his or her choice to record council meetings. We did not forget the reality of what he had done, but we complied with the appeal's results. One of the parents on the council was fearful that we would be sued because he had just bought a house. I was not fearful; I literally had nothing to lose.

A similar situation for me, not having to do with the busing court-order, but in reverse, happened about thirty years later, about 2005. By that time my children were full adults and I had all those years of teaching and administrative experience in schools and had fully considered what equal education meant by then. My work has always been about helping students to be their own best selves. The situation in question was one of those unfortunate occasions when my last name deceitfully gave me entry as a supposed person of color when I was not. Somehow my name ended up on an email list of concerned parents and educators in the Boston Public Schools who were planning a program to help narrow the achievement gap between diverse students. Thinking that maybe my experiences could be of some help to the group, I responded positively to their invitation. When I arrived at the meeting site, the participants (all black) just stared at me. I asked where I might sign in, and they referred me to a woman in another room. She was alone in there and started asking me questions about how I knew about the meeting and why I was there. She was not rude about it, but informed me that it was a closed group and apologized that they had misled me into believing that I would be welcome. I started to explain that my children were black but decided not to as it would not have made any difference. I left. Sometimes a white mother in a bi-racial family does not belong anywhere! Although I can understand the possibility of my being a spy from the school department for all they knew, it was not a pleasant experience. How often does that kind of thing happen to black folks? Probably all the time, but hopefully not as often as it used to.

One of the benefits of the busing court order, at least for me, was the "experts" that were brought in to enlighten us about racism. One particular professor from Boston University told us that when incidents arise, and someone after the fact says it was a racist event then **IT IS**. Whether or not both parties agree, if one of them feels that he or she has been singled out as less-than, that feeling defines the situation as racist and should, ideally, be thoroughly discussed by the participants. That insight has stayed with me all these forty years and has often helped me unpack the complexities of such events. Situations like the story about the parent council meeting may seem matter-of-fact and straightforward, but the hidden under-currents make it a racist event. I noted that black parents knew exactly what was happening, while it was happening, whereas I did not. In that council meeting, one side of the disagreement was presented by an all-white group. All people of color were on the other side, with some white allies like me, but still outnumbered. When there are two groups in a disagreement, with one side predominantly from one race and the other side from another race, those conditions can lead to a racist event. As a society and as individuals, we only seem to make progress toward racial understanding in small increments. And sometimes there is a deterioration of understanding. Which is why we are all only "thus far on the way." All these twists and turns on the pathway can be agonizing.

The process of busing itself did not directly affect us as a family until the boys left the Ohrenberger after fifth grade. Dan and Bruce both went on to an advanced work class probably seven or eight miles from our home and you can find their views of those years in Chapter 13. There was a mixture of races among the students on their school bus. They sometimes had to ride under the bus seats for protection from rocks aimed at its windows. This was fully five years after busing had started. It was a fearful time for all parents, and we Kihanyas were no exception when our children became the targets. We were still determined that they get the best education that public schools could give them. That bus ride was the price to be paid for participating in the advanced class. Their vulnerability probably bothered me more than them. Fortunately, they never got hurt. At least not physically. Later, when Ed left fifth grade, five years later, he was not eligible for an advanced class because of his learning challenges. We scraped together the money and sent him to a Catholic school out of the city.

One fun thing we did as a family to clear our minds of the battlefield in Boston was to take our first big vacation in 1978. All five of us drove the length of U.S. Route 95 from Boston to Florida, ending at Disney World. While we had our trusty maps to guide us, what they did not tell us was where we could safely stop along the way for food and gas.

Safely, as in what areas we could be sure that we would not be harassed for our family's composition. There were no guarantees anyway. We did not have any problems until late one evening, somewhere in North Carolina, we were running out of gas and there was no choice but to stop. We pulled off the highway and approached the first service station that we saw. The attendant was a white fellow who spoke with a pronounced Southern accent and sported overalls. He looked like someone from "Mayberry, R.F.D." I know, stereotyping. The fellow was probably harmless but just in case, we did not allow the boys out to use the bathroom facilities there. We used our now-full gas tank to scoot down the highway to a restaurant that was better lighted and out in the open.

We had a lot of fun at Disney World and our sons remember that trip fondly. While we enjoyed all the attractions, David could not help but remark about how few African Americans were there. He often made that same comment when we went on our weekly visits to the Boston Science Museum. He wondered what was keeping people of color from taking advantage of the educational and recreational activities that might improve their lives and those of their children. A number of factors probably contributed to the lack of participation by black parents then. As when we were at the gas station, they might not be sure they would be welcome there. And such activities may not have been advertised well in the black community. We can be sure that black parents would want such activities for their children just as much as white parents did and do. The last time I visited Disney World the numbers of black visitors had increased but was still not in tune with their percentage in the population of the U. S. or even of Florida.

One could never really say that busing in Boston was "successful." Did it succeed in integrating the children and promoting diversity? Yes. Did it equalize the resources spent on varying classifications (races) of students? Yes. Did it improve education in the system?

Maybe for some, but certainly not all. Did it improve race relations in the city? Certainly not, initially, but perhaps over the course of years. As Martin Luther King once said, "People fail to get along because they fear each other; they fear each other because they don't know each other; they don't know each other because they have not communicated with each other."

Marriage of Anne Whitaker & Richard Simpson, Grannell Family, 1987

"The service you do for others is the rent you pay for your room here on Earth."

— Muhammad Ali

SEVEN – MULTICULTURAL EDUCATION, 1979-87

Out of the partnership between the Ohrenberger School and Emmanuel College, there emerged the position of Multicultural Coordinator for the school. Later on it became a district-wide position. I was chosen to fill the opening. Some of the strengths that may have led to my hiring were my investment in the school as a parent, my own multicultural lifestyle, my college degree, and an avid interest in the subject matter. And yes, as I see it now, my whiteness. The teachers on the task force had been working on a basic grade-level curriculum which was to be expanded year by year. It began by encouraging students to share "All About Me." It continued with human and civil rights questions and expanded to the specific information about the cultures represented in the student population. While it did eventually include units on gender equality, it had none on sexual orientation. It likely would in this day and age.

From 1978 through 1987 I produced the curriculum materials for the homeroom teachers, invited speakers and performers to elaborate on the curriculum and planned the celebration of various cultural and ethnic holidays. The holiday celebrations were meant to be a way to acknowledge differences and find joy in each other. I believe now that we were a bit naïve about that. There was an amazing array of cultures at the school. The BPS bilingual program for Laotians was housed there, so we celebrated Laotian New Year in April. One quarter of the building was designated for students with multiple physical and mental challenges, so we designed a unit on disabilities. There was a sizeable population of Jewish students. Whatever designation a student's family identified with, we addressed. We celebrated Rosh Hoshanah, Laotian and Chinese New Year, Martin Luther King Day, Black History Month and June 'Teenth, St. Patrick's Day, Boxing Day, Kwanzaa, Three Kings' Day, Columbus Day (not sure we would have that now), Greek Independence Day, Harvest festivals, and holidays common to all –

Thanksgiving, Arbor Day, New Year's Day (January 1). We produced a calendar to help us remember which holidays were when, with monthly pictures drawn by the students. And in the spring, we had an "International Fair" where we shared ethnic foods, dancing and singing, national flags, and artwork, and we raised funds then to improve and expand the programming.

I learned more about human relations, racial relations and ethnic and racial pride during this period than I did in any other period of my life. I definitely learned even more than the students did. I had to study and research in order to assist the teachers in curriculum development. While I can still remember dates of most of the ethnic holidays, those were not the most important items for my own multicultural knowledge. The program made me <u>realize</u> – or make it more real – that a sense of self, of dignity, of pride and joy in our individual ethnicities, is essential to our success as human beings, and as neighbors who can understand each other. The program was a vehicle for all of us to encourage and celebrate each one's self-awareness and sense of pride in his/her heritage. My path to understanding was pretty much straight at that time.

Perhaps the single most helpful training I undertook to start the Multicultural Coordinator position was how to keep track of racial balance – in every situation. How to be vigilant about including a diversity of people in all situations. How to recognize that someone might say, "Why isn't there someone in the picture that looks like me, has freckles like me, is tall or short like me, is dark skinned or light like me?" In regard to television, books, magazines or movies, it is important that those who live in isolated situations, as I did as a child, see a representation of those unlike them – maybe the only form of interaction for them. Some form of reference before going out to meet the greater world.

As a white person in 1980's Boston, I definitely could not assume that everything was balanced. At the beginning, I had to resort to numbers as a measure of equality, but now I automatically recognize inequality without counting. For instance, when I look now at the "Dick and Jane" series that I learned to read with, there was no one who looked like my sons. I learned to look at a picture and question the ethnic, racial and gender makeup of those portrayed, and to question why this or that kind of person was not there. The Garrity court order itself required that the schools safeguard fair inclusionary practices and that was also initially achieved by counting. This counting and awareness practice keeps me observant about diversity and inclusion to this day. It matters that people of all backgrounds have a chance to learn and to contribute in a group. That ads on television are representative of the whole audience. That young people have an equal chance to participate equally in sports, in school, everywhere. That college application materials have pictures of all who should be welcomed there. Furthermore, I am still almost always aware of the racial, gender, ethnic and sexual orientation of those in the room – and what role to play in making everyone feel welcome and included. That was a lesson that has served me well.

The Multicultural Program office was located just off the school library and volunteer center where a population of diverse parents assisted the librarian and the Multicultural Program. Being ensconced in that setting, I had free access to a wealth of elementary-level books about all aspects of black culture. The books – and the richness of their content – were a pleasure that I reveled in. And they contributed to my own growing knowledge of black culture.

My tenure as Multicultural Coordinator was a fruitful period in my life, even though this also was the beginning of David's and my separation and divorce. The multicultural and multiracial parents and teachers working with me on the Multicultural program, became dear, lifelong friends who have taught me more than I deserve to know about communication between persons with differences. We shared a sense of purpose and a willingness to be honest with each other. We were collectively interested in the growth of kind-hearted acceptance among the children and adults. We learned to work together as equals. We did not hesitate to gently correct each other about misperceptions or outright racist thinking and focused on recognizing that each person was the best expert on his or her own life, ethnicity, and self-image. Other folks were patient, as I learned to not try telling them who they were. There was no condescension among us; we were working to level the playing field. We enjoyed each other's company and even found humor within our work. I am grateful for the sharing we did then and for the habit of listening that I haven't entirely mastered even now.

Cousins on Chebeague, 1981 – Meghan Mulholland (standing), Mark Whitaker, Susan Grannell, Maureen Mulholland

"Looking at life from a different perspective makes you realize that it's not the deer that is crossing the road but rather the road that is crossing the forest."

– Muhammad Ali

EIGHT – CHEBEAGUE ISLAND

My unbroken ancestral line shows one strand that has now enjoyed a beautiful island in Casco Bay, Maine, for eleven generations, including my children and grandchildren. Chebeague Island has been home to Hamiltons and Grannells, and now to Whitakers, Kihanyas, Mulhollands, Sawyers, Terrells, Herricks, Maksouds, Soravillas, Simpsons, Cegalis', Pastores, Pogodzienskis and Johnsons – since the 1750's. The Grannell family homestead, "Grannell Cottage," was built about 1880 and stands proudly on North Road today. It is not grandiose in any way, and more likely would be dubbed folksy and comfortable.

The original settlers on the island, in the seventeen and eighteen hundreds, were the Native summer people who named it "Jebeg," or "The Land of Many Springs." Later came the year-round settlers who were my ancestors, Ambrose Hamilton and his wife Deborah Soule. The Hamiltons had fourteen children and seventy-seven grandchildren, so we have many, many relatives among the approximately 350 year-round residents. The young people in our family have made friends there over the years, only to find out that they were actually distant cousins. Some were very surprised that Dan, Bruce and Ed were related to them.

One particular place on the island has both a spiritual and a nostalgic feel to it – the United Methodist Church, at this time the only church there. My great-great grand-mother was one of the founding members and I find such peace as I sit through services, listening to the word and realizing my family's rich tradition there. The church's décor has changed little in its 160 years of existence – wood-paneled walls, narrow pews and a large cross-stitched copy of the Lord's Prayer on the wall. And, oh yes, the cemetery right out the window, the resting place of so many in the family, including my parents and two siblings.

In 1975, my father, George Grannell, became the sole owner of the house, its antique furnishings, its family documents and pictures, and its surrounding land. Before his death in 1987, he ceded the property to a non-profit corporation, controlled by his five children. Now it is managed by twelve stockholders, most of whom are Dad's grandchildren. All of this is to say that we all have the right to enjoy the property, by weekly registration, every summer, and almost all of us (some in-laws would disagree) love our time there.

Our sons were very young when we first started going there. I had only ever visited there once before that. The property had never been legally probated before 1975, and my Dad's cousin lived there, but only in summer at that point. His lifestyle was not one that Dad wanted us to see. We Kihanyas and Grannells brought some of the first color to the population, although Native Americans were there long before us. Maine was predominantly white then, and the Chebeague population was even whiter. Maine is still the second whitest state in the nation.

It was, and is, a wonderful place for anyone to vacation, but especially for children. They could ride bikes anywhere and be safe, both from traffic and from the crime of the mainland. Available to them were swim lessons, sailing lessons, tennis lessons and golf lessons. They picked berries, played croquet, Frisbee and badminton, and built rafts and treehouses. They walked to Vacation Bible School up the road. A very happy place for boys from the city.

The rainbow of children in our front yard made us all feel blessed. My sons and their African American cousins blended right in with the Florida and Massachusetts cousins. And they did and do take that for granted. All of the nieces and nephews, and now their spouses and children, treat multi-racial situations as no big deal because they have always been used to it. In the 1970's and 80's, they each found a bed in the house that they claimed as theirs and they willingly sat at the children's table out on the deck while the grownups sat in the dining room for dinner. Most of those little ones are parents themselves now and bring their own children to enjoy those same activities. They are still close and work together to ensure that the property is maintained and ready for their grandchildren when that time comes.

My grandson Michael recently wrote the following for a school essay. It seems to sum up what we all feel about our time on the island. "The world disappears when I take the boat to the island from the mainland. The clear skies, clean streets, and stillness relax me, making me less worried and anxious. The beauty of the island makes it a place where you are meant to find peace. The lack of technology on the island makes it seem to a younger generation like an ancient city. To me, it is the lack of connection to the outside world that fosters a deeper connection to those who you currently have around you. The smartphone that usually distracts me fades away and is tucked into a pocket of my backpack for hours at a time, without a second thought. The lack of Snapchat gives me an opportunity to do chores with my Uncle

Andy. Instead of blankly scrolling through my Instagram feed I can chat with my cousin about her nursing degree. I can go on hikes through the woods with my grandpa and my father, appreciating the beauty. I can win a long jump competition against my sister on the beach. The entire time being present in the experience."

One aspect of our summer visits to the island that has always been confusing is the differentiation between the year 'rounders and those who they refer to as "the summer complaint." We Grannells are never really sure which camp we belong in. We certainly don't live there in January but on the other hand, our people have been there for about 350 years and more than twenty-five of us are buried in the graveyard. We contribute to the church there and attend services there all summer. I personally visit the island's website daily all year to keep up with the various non-profits that we participate in. We are close enough family that the islanders share with us their jokes. It is said that the island rises up an inch on Labor Day when the summer people leave!

Having always wanted to share the Chebeague experience with others, I have invited many friends to visit for a day or two, over the years. And in fact, many of those visitors were African American. In 1992, as a teacher of sixth grade at St. Joseph's School in Roxbury, I invited my class and two chaperones to spend Memorial Day weekend on the island. We had a grand time! We left on Friday so that we could visit the island school that afternoon. Together there, we developed a Venn diagram of the similarities and differences between the Boston and the Chebeague youngsters, then went outside to play softball. It was interesting to see the interactions between the two groups.

The next day it was too cold for swimming, but they roamed the beaches collecting shells, driftwood and stones for souvenirs. We also visited the local gift shop, where one student was shocked to hear the proprietor tell him to take a bag and select the candy he wanted. He was not used to being trusted like that. We went for a walk in the woods and saw a fox which terrified several of them.

They all were required to keep a journal while they were there, to record both their activities and impressions. It was obvious from their writing that they may as well have been in a foreign country. They were so overwhelmed by the differences from their daily lives. They spoke of the calming spirit of the place, its scenery, and its people who wave to everybody. They mentioned how fortunate they thought my family was, to be able to go there all the time. About fifteen years later, I encountered one of the students who had gone to the island that weekend, and she said that was her favorite memory from that school year, and that she still was hoping that she could do something like that for a city child herself. She is now a lawyer in Washington D.C. For me that weekend retreat is a very special memory of Chebeague!

One funny story about Chebeague

happened about 1980. We were at the ferry landing across the bay waiting for a return trip to the island. My sister-in-law Dorothy, mother of two African American children, David, and I sat on some boulders while our five children played below at the water's edge. We noticed some whispering and staring going on among some vacationers around us and decided to have some fun at their expense. Not nice, but funny all the same. David was leaving directly from there, and the rest of us were staying on for another week. He climbed down and said goodbye to all the children and came back up and kissed both Dorothy and I with gusto! Thus, it appeared that he was father to all the children and husband/partner to the two of us! Good fun while reminding others that our lives were not their business and it could be even "worse" than they imagined!

On a more serious note, that incident did have some relevance to a cultural difference I had with David. In his tribe, in the past, it was common for a man to be polygamous. In fact, his own father had two wives for a while. When we were finally able to buy a house after thirteen years of marriage, David decided that he wanted to buy two houses: a fixer-upper that he would live in and a ranch house that the boys and I would live in, around the corner. This seemed a little too close to his Kikuyu tradition of having multiple wives living in a circle of homes in which the husband would inhabit the main house and each wife would have her own hut to live in with her children. And the father would move from hut to hut, "visiting." I never knew, nor would he say, if David was doing this on purpose or not, but I had reached my limit in accommodating our differences, and we separated legally. The beginning of the end. I stayed in our apartment with the boys and he moved to his master house, renting out the other. Our differences were entirely cultural. Not racial differences as our detractors would have you believe.

Chebeague Island and its residents have always been so welcoming! I am not aware of a single instance of racist behavior in over forty years I have been there. Well one house did have a Confederate flag outside, but those folks only stayed a couple of years. The island was much, much more colorful in its summer population in 2018 than it was in 1975. One can no longer assume that an African American vacationer is probably staying at Grannell Cottage. Chebeague has been one of the only places where my family always feels comfortable. Family, peace, no judgment. And no "color line." Just us.

Easter in Rumford, 1969

"I think it is one of the tragedies of our nation, one of the shameful tragedies, that eleven o'clock on Sunday morning is one of the most segregated hours, if not the most segregated hours, in Christian America."
– Dr. Martin Luther King Jr. April 17, 1960

NINE – CHURCH LIFE, 1966-2019

Church attendance in the United States has been racially segregated since the 1600's. The Pilgrims and Puritans were exclusively Caucasian, and most came to this country to practice a particular religious belief. Therefore, whatever Native peoples, or others of color, were around were not invited to worship, or maybe would not have wanted to attend anyway. In the time of slavery, the Africans were not invited to organized churches because it was erroneously believed that those they had enslaved did not have souls. In the North that was somewhat different so that, for instance, Phillis Wheatley, the African American poet, attended church at predominantly white Old South Church in Boston in the 1770's and 80's. Even when slavery became illegal, many white church goers, especially in the South, were afraid of the possibility that any mixing of races at any activity would lead to mixed-race children. Never mind that slaveholders had been fur- thering "miscegenation" for many generations. The segregation pattern in churches was set early and seems to remain even now.

People are apt to attend religious services with those they feel most comfortable, and they usually feel more comfortable with those of a like or similar ethnic and racial background. That practice would seem to exclude families like mine, trying to stay balanced on the "color line." Distance is another factor in church choice; people prefer a church that is close by. Since many neighborhoods are segregated, as they have been in Boston, so are the churches. Wikipedia reports that, "As many as 87% of Christian churches in the United States are completely made up of only white or only African-American parishioners in 2018."

In the nearly sixty years since Martin Luther King spoke of the segregation of Christian churches in our country, the situation still has not changed much. These years follow the same timeline as my immersion in African American culture. Our family chose carefully where we would attend church. It was a very important decision for us both since David and I are both serious Christians (David's father was a lay preacher in the Presbyterian Church in Kenya).

I am a lifelong United Methodist and my son Ed, is an eighth generation Methodist. Once again, a reminder to me of our unbroken ancestral line. My family was in the Methodist movement all the way back to its beginnings with founder John Wesley in England in the 1770's. John Wesley himself was an anti-slavery activist, and a supporter of William Wilberforce's anti-slave-trade movement. He was also the author of a book named Thoughts Upon Slavery (1774), in which he said, "Here it may not be necessary to repeat what has been fully declared in several modern publications of the inconsistence of slavery with every right of mankind, with every feeling of humanity, and every precept of Christianity; nor to point out its inconsistency with the welfare, peace and prosperity of every country, in proportion as it prevails; what grievous sufferings it brings on the poor Negroes; but more especially what a train of fatal vices it produces in their lordly oppressors and their unhappy off-spring."

In a mission that addressed both his religious and his social beliefs, Wesley sailed to Georgia, in America, specifically to invite enslaved Africans and the so-called "Indians" to become Christians. Although he remained for two years, his mission was a failure and he returned to England.

The history of my church, and of my family, is intertwined and I am inordinately proud of it. But one aspect where my pride falls away again is the history of segregated Methodist churches in the South and even in Philadelphia in the past. Still and all, a complete history shows that John Wesley was not interested in establishing a homogenous church; rather, he wanted people of all backgrounds to know God. And for sure all Methodist churches throughout the world today are open to all from any race though sadly some, mostly outside the

United States, are not open to LBGTQ inclusion.

One belief in the United Methodist Church that has had a profound effect on my growing understanding of racial politics is found in the denomination's <u>Social Principles</u> under "The Nurturing Community:"

'The Church is called to challenge and recreate cultural norms within the Church itself and in any social context where dominant norms are used to legitimate the superiority of one culture over another. We seek to guard the unity of humanity, while honoring God's gift of diversity (I Cor. 9:17; 12:7, NRSV).'

These thoughts and biblical understandings have supported me throughout the years. Being a Methodist has not only enriched my spiritual and biblical understanding but has also showed me the ways that my life can conform to the Gospel. In addition, I am very proud to be an active member of United Methodist Women, an organization in mission for 150 years now, serving women, children and youth throughout the world. This is why I have remained a Methodist.

As a family, the Kihanyas were searching for a church home in the 1960's, when many black churches were heavily involved in the Civil Rights movement. It seemed ideal for a family like ours to find such a church that would combine the two emphases of Martin Luther King: Christianity and African American progress toward civil rights. At the same time, neither David nor I had any real knowledge of the black neighborhoods of Boston, or of the churches there. There were neither Anglican (David's preference) nor Methodist churches near our home. So, we spent about five years visiting churches here and there, never finding what we were looking for. And missing church on many Sundays.

In 1973 we had just moved to still another neighborhood when we discovered a Methodist Church not too far away and so I moved my membership from the Rumford church for the first time – to Bethany United Methodist Church in Roslindale. It was a predominantly white church then, but that factor bothered me more than it did David. The boys were in Sunday School there until they each graduated from high school. I taught Sunday School and participated in several of the administrative committees and Project A.C.T.S. (see below). One adult there did advise me that our son Dan had told her that I was not really his mother and that his real mother was in Kenya. Dan denied it vehemently and I believed him. The teller of the tale was a well-known gossip. She may have been fishing for our personal information. We were happy to pursue our religious life at Bethany Church and David is still a member there and the congregation is much, much more diverse now.

While we were attending the Roslindale church, they were participating in an ecumenical social action experiment named Project A.C.T.S. (Association of Churches for Training and Service). The idea was to have both Protestant and Catholic churches in

Roslindale and Hyde Park neighborhoods work together to improve life for residents of the area. Each church chose an improvement area to work on. We chose transportation needs and I volunteered to chair our task force. A community organizer guided us through the process. In an initial survey we found that there was a need for public transportation from the Roslindale section of the city down to Dudley Station in the Roxbury section. In other words, a direct bus line between the white and black neighborhoods.

We began the process by knocking on doors all along the proposed route and surveying residents about their transportation needs. We also asked what their opinion was of the proposed route. They were invited to sign a petition to the Massachusetts Bay Transportation Authority requesting that such a route be established. There was a more positive reaction at the Roxbury end of the line than there was in Roslindale, but this was the time of school busing in Boston and the word "bus" was not at all popular. Those who were interested, and even excited about the idea, spoke of how much easier it would be to get to their favorite laundromat, to visit relatives and to shop and seek employment. Those who were opposed to the idea spoke of not wanting people to wait at a bus stop near their house, and how it would probably invite an undesirable population to their part of town.

The second part of the process was to hold a series of community meetings in which residents would have a chance to ask questions and state opinions. Each church asked its congregants to attend meetings for all the projects in order to support each other. Also invited were news writers, politicians, business owners, non-profit managers and other community leaders. One very popular local City Councilor told us that we were "doomed to fail" because the MBTA had already overspent their annual budget. And then there was the City Councilor from the other end of the proposed bus line who stated, "The buses would be important because they would unite a number of communities that have never interacted before." We were determined to win!

The final part of the process was supposed to have been our going to state politicians (MBTA is a state agency) to make our plea. We decided to dispense with talking to local representatives who would not have very much leverage to enact our proposal. Our research told us that the head of the Massachusetts Senate's Transportation Committee just happened to represent Roxbury and he **did** have the clout to make it happen. In the end, our appeal to him was successful! He took our proposal to his committee and they endorsed it. We announced the new route from the front steps of our church. It made headlines in the local newspaper and we were delighted. Within six months there was a new bus route in town. As one could only imagine, those who were opposed to it were not happy, but the politician who tried to discourage us at the hearing came back to congratulate us. And life became just a bit easier for commuters and shoppers on both ends of the line. The whole process took about eighteen months.

Roslindale is more integrated now. The percentage of African American residents in that section of town for 1990 was 8%; for 2000 it was 16%; and for 2010, 25.3% (U.S. Census). Did the new bus have anything to do with those increases? We have no proof what effect that the new inter-neighborhood bus-line had on these statistics, but those numbers still excite and encourage me. It is possible that school busing could account for some people feeling more at home in different neighborhoods, in those same time frames, but we cannot be sure. It was just an MBTA bus route yet so much more. It eased the path for many who wanted the advantages that were available in white residential zones but seldom in black neighborhoods.

After David and I separated, I went back to searching for a church. When Ed was home from college one summer, we visited Parkway United Methodist Church in Milton and found what we both thought was the perfect church for us. As noted above, it is still unusual to find a multiracial church, but that is what we found there. Its history included the fact that there was a fairly new black pastor (Caribbean-American) in what before-hand had been a mostly white congregation. Some parishioners left when he came, but even more parishioners, predominantly black and Caribbean, joined. At the present time the church is 39% Caribbean-American, 25% African American, 15% African emigres, 8% Hispanic, 8% white, and 5% multiracial. It was and is a vibrant parish, active, activist and in mission to tell the world about God. A series of pastors with varying styles and messages have challenged us with biblically based sermons. A special pleasure for me is that the very pastor who led the Bethany Church through Project A.C.T.S. those many years ago is once again our pastor at Parkway UMC. We love the music – some traditional, and some gospel, an eclectic mix that feeds our souls. We presently live in the church's neighborhood (Ed and I). We finally found a church with both the sociological and the theological identity that we had been looking for so long. We were and are very "comfortable" in that situation, especially at eleven o'clock on Sunday morning! We both enjoy the company and activities of the congregants; anyone from any background is made to feel welcome. It offers ministry and mission in so many areas: a food pantry, a health ministry, an active Religion and Race Committee and United Methodist Men's and United Methodist Women's programming. The perfect place for us!

One example of how I continue to learn about black folks through my church life happened in 2016. My good friend, Dr. Patti O'Brien Richardson, author of <u>Purge It With Patti</u>, and a former teacher with me at GED Plus (see Chapter 12), spoke to the "Women Strong" luncheon at Parkway, presenting her dissertation research on black girls, and how their hair affects their lives. She posited that many of these girls were physically inactive because they did not want to mess up their expensive and time-consuming hairdos. The result of this inactivity is that while they maintain their hairdos, their physical health begins to deteriorate, and they gain weight. Patti has been a professor at Rutgers and taught a course on this topic there. Hair is definitely a topic to be taken seriously by any African American, male or female. Both my children and my grandchildren began life with big loopy curls and gradually advanced to their now tighter curls. While some white women are fascinated by and somewhat jealous of curly hair, care of that hair is often difficult, and as I said, expensive to maintain.

Not touching an African American's hair was another lesson that I had to learn from someone who cared enough to caution me about it. While white women believe that it is a compliment to touch and exclaim about African American hair, it is not received that way among those who have it. So, even when the touching is not meant to be demeaning and intrusive, it feels that way to bearer of the hair.

We have a picture in our multiracial family

of an African American mother (my niece) arranging her two-year-old daughter's hair while a blond boy cousin is checking out the feel of the hair with a brush. So, the curiosity starts pretty young. These two are young adults now and still as close as ever, but I don't think he tries to touch her hair like that anymore. Live and learn and remember. For all of us.

Grandchildren of George and Edna Grannell, Chebeague, 1981

"Education then, beyond all other devices of human origin, is the great equalizer of the conditions of men, the balance-wheel of the social machinery."

— Horace Mann

TEN – CURRY COLLEGE 1988-90

From 1987-1990, having completed my role as Multicultural Coordinator, I served as the full-time building substitute teacher for the Ohrenberger School. Within that time frame, from 1988-1990, I pursued a Masters' degree in Reading Education at Curry College in Milton, Massachusetts. Curry had initiated a program that would admit a cohort of twenty-five BPS teachers who wanted to work on a Masters' Degree in Education. The class met together every Wednesday afternoon, and most weekends, for two years. The courses were offered at a reduced price, so the opportunity and the concept attracted me immediately. As a permanent substitute teacher, I was selected to participate.

Going back to school was the best thing I ever did for myself. I thrived there, unlike in undergrad days when I felt the pressure of parental sacrifices, the lack of a tangible goal and a long-term homesickness. And then marriage and motherhood. At Curry my learning could be simultaneously applied to my daily work. At the same time, I did not have a lot of distractions at home by then. There was never a question of why we were learning these things. Our daily work life made it obvious.

Our professor was also our advisor. From the beginning she prepared us for the thesis that we would have to produce before graduation. Almost none of us knew each other before the classes started but got to know each other very well during our time together. Among the twenty-five participants were maybe five African Americans.

From the beginning, we were encouraged to think about what kind of project, what research hypothesis we would like to pursue. By the end of the first year I had begun research on how violence in their communities might be affecting my students' behavior, and their ability to concentrate on learning. My proposal abstract stated: "The purpose of this study was to develop a bibliotherapeutic whole language instructional model that addresses the emotions of urban third graders, relieves and releases their stress, and preserves valuable instructional time."

Bibliotherapy is a procedure that uses discussion about literature to process emotional stress, in this case the stress visited on those who experience violence. In its more extreme form, this is the Post Traumatic Stress Disorder that often affects soldiers returning from war. Over the course of a short teaching career I had worked with elementary students who were living with the aftermath of violence that took many forms. Following are a few examples:

- A ten-year-old girl who had witnessed her father murdering her mother when she was five

- An eight-year-old boy who slept under his bed, which was necessitated by the sound of gun shots nearby and a bullet that became lodged in the siding outside his window

- Another ten-year-old whose mother had beaten her so badly that her skull had been fractured; she was now in foster care

- A kindergartener who at nap time literally slept with his eyes open, because his teenage sister had been shot right outside their house

While those were a few of the stories that we staff knew about, there were many more that were obvious, but details were not available to us. There were students whose behavior included self-isolation from fellow students, falling asleep at their desks daily, or continually appearing disheveled and unwashed. All these signaled serious problems in their homes and/or neighborhoods, some of it violent. This was a time when the murder rate in Boston was at its height. While the annual murder rate for Boston from 2002-2014 averaged 59 per year, the rate for the years 1980-1989 was 92; in fact, in the year 1990 it unfortunately reached an historic 143. (Boston Police Department statistics) Unfortunately these murders were pre-dominantly in the black community. Every such Boston murder affects some BPS student, and more likely many, since the victims are mostly young.

The literature I selected to use in the proposed curriculum included such old-fashioned but violent stories as "Little Red Riding Hood" and the poem "Humpty Dumpty," up to more recent but scary stories such as "Where the Wild Things Are." There were also those that dealt with violence and death directly: "Everett Anderson's Good-bye" and "The Fall of Freddie the Leaf." All the stories were selected for their potential to elicit student experience and feelings about violence. Because the students who were dealing with violence were predominantly (but certainly not exclusively) students of color, I included many stories about African American children.

One of my fellow Masters' students and I worked closely together, even though our projects were very different. We researched in libraries all over the greater Boston area. It was still a time when, to do research, you had to talk to research librarians, use the Dewey Decimal system, and sit for hours flipping through old newspaper and magazine stories in a back room. It is so much easier now when facts and stories are right at your fingertips on the internet. One advantage of us working together was that we could apprise each other about research that we would come across that would fit into the other's thesis. And we could enjoy our rides together between research sites. She was still one more person in my life who taught me what not to say and what not to do that would insult and/or aggravate African Americans.

Unfortunately, the bibliotherapy curriculum was never fully implemented because the very next fall after graduation I switched to teaching in Catholic Schools where their curriculum was already set. I did use parts of it from time to time, but it would be difficult to measure its effectiveness on a part-time basis. When I did use it, the student response was positive and sparked conversations that were encouraging to me. Pursuing a Masters' degree in this way and with these results endures as one of my favorite activities ever.

Boston Student Visiting on Chebeague

"The life of a teacher, as I know from personal experience, is very challenging and demanding, but it is also profoundly satisfying. It is more than a job, for it is rooted in our deepest convictions and values."

— Pope John Paul II

ELEVEN – TEACHING IN CATHOLIC SCHOOLS 1990-99

My belief in the importance of racial balance in employment was well-formed before the Boston Public Schools denied me employment after I finished my Masters' Degree at Curry. The busing court order included a requirement that one black teacher had to be hired for every white teacher hired. While affirmative action has been out of favor among some who feel that it gives an unfair advantage to minorities and women, I believe that the action is necessary to at least partially counteract the disadvantages visited on those minorities in historical discrimination. In any case there have been other methods and styles of affirmative action for a very long time now, in the form of, for instance, legacy admissions to colleges or nepotism in many firms. Affirmative action is also meant to ensure that public employees represent the people that they serve, in the BPS case, students. Still today, 87% of Boston Schools' students are children of color whereas only 37% of their teachers are persons of color. (teachboston.org)

It was right for me philosophically to espouse affirmative action, but that was difficult to reconcile with my desire for a paycheck commensurate with my educational level. I wanted to find some way to get into the Boston school system, mostly because it paid better. In the end, I was never hired there, because the newly reduced number of white positions available were taken by those with political connections. Not entirely, but it was definitely a factor. My connections were flimsy at best. One white BPS teacher even advised me to claim I was from a bi-racial family; she thought that might get me in! That would have been wrong in so many ways. My beliefs were challenged, but I continued to support the one-for-one rule, even when it affected me adversely.

One job application experience in this period was again about my last name. I applied for a position at Boston University that appeared to be offered through the office of former Mayor Kevin White, and I was invited for an interview. When the ex-mayor came into the waiting area to escort me into his office, he exclaimed, "Are **YOU** Kathryn Kihanya?" He was obviously surprised that the complexion of my face did not seem to match the name on my resume. There was nothing on that resume that would have identified me as African American except the name. You know what they say about people who make assumptions! I did not get the job. So, I took another turn in the road and applied to Catholic schools. I really believe now that I was supposed to do that in life. Even now, with a tiny pension; yes, the court order was right!

The first Catholic School that hired me was St. Andrew's, in Jamaica Plain, probably the most diverse neighborhood in Boston. The principal was a good-natured and pleasant nun from the Sisters of Charity of New Jersey. The teaching staff was about half from that same religious order and the other half lay teachers. We were a tight-knit group and I remain very close friends with those lay teachers all these years later. The nuns have all passed away, and some of our lay friends also. While the staff was all white, the students were mixed, with about twenty percent either African American, Hispanic American or Asian-American. The immediate neighborhood had been white for a long time but was in the process of transitioning to greater diversity in 1990.

I taught grades seven and eight and not surprisingly was not allowed to teach religion. Having taught at all levels over the years, I know that middle school age is the toughest to deal with and these students were no exception. The rules at St. Andrew's were strict as compared to public school. And too, there loomed the threat of expulsion, which of course was not a factor in public school. At the same time, I only ever witnessed one expulsion in nine years in Catholic Schools, and that was ordered by the priest in charge of the church there, and not by the teacher or principal. Still and all, that threat was a real possibility.

Among the students in my first year at the school was a boy who came to my class for seventh grade history while the nun in their homeroom taught my eighth graders religion. The boy was white – this factor will be important later – and let's call him "Jimmy" (not his real name). So, one day "Jimmy" was seated at his desk next to me and facing the rest of the class because he had been disrupting the lesson. We were at the end of class, and the students were waiting to return to their homeroom. They were waiting patiently, when suddenly, there was a noise next to me. Everybody laughed raucously, even the students who did not usually exhibit unruly behavior. I ignored the noise. Again, "click-click." So, I turned to "Jimmy" and asked him to give me whatever was making the noise. After trying to pretend that it wasn't him, he passed me what appeared to be a lighter. Later, I knew how sensible I had been to put it away without inspecting it further. When I did check it, and clicked it as he had, out popped a plastic penis! I did not think it was funny then, but I do now. I tell this story as an example of "Jimmy's" behavior.

When it came time for our first parent open house of the year, I was nervous. I had never participated in a parent-teacher conference, except on the parent end. My sister advised me that I would be alright as long as I didn't meet myself across the desk! She knew that I was infamous for confronting teachers when I felt that my sons were treated unfairly. I may be the mother of bi-racial children but that did not deter me from using my white privilege training on their behalf!

The first parent to appear that night was "Jimmy's" mother and she was very unhappy with his grades. She appeared to be someone who did not care much about herself or her children. Judgment, I know, but her look was slovenly. She wore a soiled tee shirt, the arm of which was folded back over a cigarette pack. It sounds like a stereotype but is really how she presented herself. I did not mention the lighter incident to her.

I tried to talk to her about his poor home-work record, his lack of class participation and his disruptive behavior. She interrupted me at one point and said, "You know, don't you, that he only acts like that because of your situation." Initially I did not realize what she was talking about, but then I suddenly knew what she was insinuating. So, I made her say it, asking, "What situation is that?" She replied, "You know, your family." Trying to remain calm, I told her that if that was a factor, then the whole class would be acting up, and that was not the case. I then reviewed with her what "Jimmy's" seven-year history in the school had been like. All she said after that was that I had no right to see his past records, although of course I did.

The principal came to me after the open house was over, as she had heard what happened with "Jimmy's" mother. She was apologetic and upset over it all, but I reassured her that it was not her fault. Or the school's for that matter. There was evidently a very dysfunctional, not to mention racist, environment in the home. That event made it difficult to teach "Jimmy" for the rest of the year, but I did manage to treat him as fairly as possible, I believe. Still it can be difficult to remain peaceful when your blood is boiling!

This story is not indicative of the day-to-day environment at St. Andrew's at all, but more indicative of the white/black overt confrontations that were rampant in Boston then. Being able to mention God there made the atmosphere feel more welcoming, calm, and more open to considering the home-life of each student. However, my time in Catholic schools reinforced my long-held observation that just because a family can afford tuition does not mean that there is no abuse, drug and alcohol overuse, or general dysfunction in the students' homes. Unfortunately for children, these factors are evident throughout our society and too often in their families.

At St. Andrew's there was none of that old story of nuns hitting students with rulers. And for me, it was a new place to use the multicultural curriculum from the Ohrenberger and also my thesis curriculum. I remember inviting the eighth graders to use the information we had just learned about Martin Luther King to turn into a rap, the music they seemed to prefer.

After two years at St. Andrew's, I moved on to St. Joseph's in Roxbury, which had a very refreshing atmosphere. I was to spend seven years there, two as a sixth-grade teacher and five as associate principal. The twin themes of the school were based on Roman Catholic Doctrine, and on the Seven Principles of Kwanzaa (*Nguzo Saba*), an African American holiday week that begins on December 26 each year. For those not familiar with Kwanzaa, the seventh principle, for instance, is Imani (faith):

"To believe, with all our heart, in our Creator, our people, our parents, our teachers, our leaders, and the righteousness and victory

of our struggle."

The language in the name of each principle is Swahili, spoken mostly in eastern Africa.

Each class was assigned one of the principles, and, for instance, since Imani is the seventh principle, and that was assigned to grade 5 or the seventh class in the school. We gathered all together as a school every morning to pray, make announcements and sing the Black National Anthem. Individual classes were in charge of the gathering, on a rotating basis. The daily class leaders often made presentations about their classwork or Black History. There were about 200 students in the eight grade levels.

Many children also participated in an out-of-school time dance class taught by a graduate of the Alvin Ailey Dance Troupe. For a year or two I conducted a writing club that was very well attended, fun and productive. I was particularly proud of the students who wrote the following rap:

I was lookin' at a movie and what did I see?
There were black people in slavery
I turned it off 'cause it was a shame
African people without their real names.
Blacks in the field, that's really sad
Workin' for white masters, makes me mad.
The message is still on your radio station
Sorry to say, racism's still in this nation.

St. Joseph's had all the advantages of being a Christian private school like St. Andrew's, and at the same time emphasizing the children's own culture and their self-esteem. The children were almost entirely African American. In my seven years in that setting there was only one white student. For the students it was a total immersion in Black History, black children's literature, black achievement and black culture in general. I learned a great deal about African American culture there. On my first day as a teacher in the sixth-grade classroom there, the students were encouraged to ask me about myself – and the first question was, "Do you like black kids?" I am sure that that boy did not expect me to laugh, but I was delighted to be in a place where it was safe to ask such a question and expect an honest answer.

The staff was a mix of races and all female. Students were taught to address the staff in two different ways: African-American staff like this: "Mama Jane," and white staff like this: "Miss Jane" The Mama designation was a leftover from a time when the school's staff had been entirely African-American. I never understood why there was the difference in addressing adults, but I did not say so out loud either. Sometimes my grandmother's admonition about not making a fuss revisits me. It made me feel like there were two tiers of adults and I was the lower one. Never a good feeling. Uncomfortable. Definitely uncomfortable.

One incident at St. Joseph that I remember vividly happened on October 2, 1995, the day of the O. J. Simpson verdict. Having followed the trial on the evening news, I was very interested in how the trial would end. I told the principal we should encourage especially the older classes to watch on television because this would be an historic event. Four of us watched the office television, two black women and two white women. The verdict was announced. We did not say a word, none of us. We all sighed and walked away, none of us trusting that we were safe in revealing our true reaction. Not unexpectedly, as I found out later, the two black women were elated and the two of us white women were disappointed. Probably predictable. But, because we cared about each other, we had not wanted to give offense.

The next day, in Dudley Square on business, I overheard a conversation in which one person said, "I don't care if he's guilty or not. Let him get off and make up for all the black men who have gone to jail for nothing." While I did not agree with letting a guilty man go free, I did understand the logic of reparations and injustice that had been voiced. For sure, on that verdict day, if not on any other, I was very white. My sense of justice encourages me to do what I can to make the playing field even for blacks and whites. But that same sense of justice makes me want to do all I can to protect women from male violence. One thing for sure, my premonition about that verdict being an historic event, and very significant and consequential in terms of race relations, rings true even today.

At St. Joseph's there was a two- or three-year-old little African American girl who would sometimes come into the office with her volunteering grandmother. We had a great rapport and she would sit in my lap when she became bored. One day, while talking to some other adult in the room about race, I offered that something or other was probably because I was white. The little girl looked up at me with her big eyes and said, "Miss Kathy, you're not white!" Then giggled. Her perception of who I was and what I looked like was like most children under five: physical traits, race in particular, don't matter and therefore don't exist. I would guess that in her now young adult years, she sees things as society expects her to. But her pronouncement was comical at the time.

The year 1994 brought many changes in my life. Our divorce was final. I became Assistant Principal, and left teaching for good. Then bought my first condominium. My children were all away at college or graduated by then. Also, in that year I was invited to spend a month in the summer at Boston University, in the African Studies Department, learning all about the continent and culture of what was then 46 countries. The selected participants were very diverse, ranging from native-born Africans to folks like me who wanted to know more about a continent that was barely mentioned in our high schools.

My desire to participate in that free course was both personal and professional. It had the potential to help me understand David's culture better. And it would certainly contribute to St. Joseph's through my proposed project: to produce units for each grade level, Kindergarten through sixth, about individual African countries, much as we had done with world-wide cultures in the Ohrenberger Multicultural program. In the end, St. Joseph's benefitted from the resulting curriculum and the "country kits" containing pictures, maps, children's books, and some artifacts and clothing for the school. Of course, my own favorite was the second grade "Kenya" unit.

One other opportunity that I enjoyed and took full advantage of was the Intercultural Training and Resource Center of the Archdiocese of Boston that operated over the course of fifteen years. There had been much finger-pointing at Catholic Schools as a convenient way out for parents trying to avoid busing in Boston. One of the ways that the Archdiocese addressed this accusation was to establish the Resource Center for teachers, in order to assist them in creating a diverse classroom atmosphere and a more inclusive curriculum. The Center provided training for teachers in matters of racial disparity and encouraged the use of African American literature by providing free books for classroom libraries. As an avid reader myself, I found it very enjoyable to share the literature with students who had not encountered it before. As an educator I improved my skills through the interactive training and discussions there.

Wedding of Karen Cassar and Bruce Kihanya, 2002 –
Extended Grannell and Kihanya Families

"We are going to build a lot more prisons if
we do not deal with the schools and their
inequalities."

– Jonathan Kozol

TWELVE – GED PLUS AT ESAC, 2001-2011

ESAC Boston, or "Ensuring Stability Through Action in the Community," was and is a Boston nonprofit agency that "strives to improve the quality of life for residents of Boston and Eastern Massachusetts" and "serves as a catalyst for strengthening neighborhoods and building communities" (agency mission statement, website). Among its programs are homeowner assistance with mortgages and needed repairs, fuel for heating homes and the GED Plus Program (now known as the ESAC Youth Opportunity Collaborative). I was hired at GED Plus in 2001 as director. The classrooms were located in Roxbury, Dorchester and Jamaica Plain, what many would call the inner-city. During my employment there, the program grew from two classes at two sites to seven classes at four sites. The student annual population grew from about thirty-five to about two hundred, and staff size grew from two to eight. Our program growth was necessitated by the burgeoning applicant demand. The

BPS dropout rate reached a high of 9.4% in the 2005-2006 school year, so we drew our population from that extensive pool of potential participants. We never advertised. Our students found us by word-of-mouth. The program's growth required gradually increased funding which we were continually seeking.

Most of the success of the program can be traced to the amazingly talented, creative and hardworking staff that made the classes run smoothly. In addition to my position, we eventually had a guidance counselor, an administrative assistant who had graduated from our program (!) and probably twelve teachers over the course of my ten years. We were fortunate in attracting young college graduates who wanted to enrich their resumes with classroom teaching experience, were very idealistic, wanting to make a difference, and very much at ease and friendly with our students. They were also reliable, clever and intelligent. The staff altogether was balanced racially, but not necessarily reflective of the student population.

The students ranged in age from sixteen to twenty-four years old, had mostly attended Boston Public Schools, and were about sixty percent male and ninety percent African American or Hispanic. They enrolled on a rolling basis, often having to take a break due to outside circumstances; they were sometimes in and out of the program five or six times before ultimately graduating or dropping out altogether. They had left school for a variety of reasons:

- expulsion for poor behavior

- not being allowed to return to BPS after incarceration by the Department of Youth Services (DYS)

- pregnancy and parenthood

- undiagnosed learning challenges

- gang involvement

- having to support their families

- frustration in academics, particularly math

- inability or unwillingness to follow the rigid attendance and behavior rules of the public school

- an overwhelming sense of hopelessness

The following poem written by a GED Plus student characterizes the conditions under which many of the students lived:

"I'm from the streets where the liquor stores are on every corner
Where peoples' moms come out to tell them get in their house
Cause they know when it get dark the thugz come out
From where the cops harass when posted up on a corner
From where dreams are hopeless and getting money is hope
I'm from where school is out and Block is in
I'm from a neighborhood wit junkies and violence
From where homeless people sleep outside covered wit newspaper
Come to where I'm from Boston where a 9 to 5 out and sellin Drugs

Is the best way to keep money in your pocket."

Some students even expressed surprise that they had lived as long as they had and were not expecting to live long enough to justify more schooling. Feeling defeated before even beginning. Probably the most motivated were the young mothers, and sometimes fathers, who suddenly realized that they had to provide for their children and would need a diploma to gain employment. I personally identified most strongly with the mothers. Not many entered the program thinking they would continue on to college, though we were able to convince some to apply and enter. Our students were products of their lifetime circumstances and still so very human, with all the potential to overcome and succeed. We were not trying to "fix" them but rather to help them find their own best selves. Our most intelligent students were often gang leaders, using their talent for organization and supervision in that way. Examples of student circumstances:

- A young man who entered the program at 17 and was still there ten years later at 27. We still were trying to help him. He was a gentle fellow who made mistake after mistake, marrying, having children, getting lost in a dead-end job, and still struggling with English as a second language. He never did graduate.

- A young woman who had a life-threatening illness, who attended classes and graduated but died soon after

- A young woman who was only fourteen when we met and was in and out of DYS (Department of Youth Services) custody; ten years later she was a new Mom and had just graduated from GED Plus and also had a plan for eventual employment

- A sixteen-year-old white entrepreneur who was incarcerated with DYS because he had been running a $2000-a-day cocaine business. He had a brilliant mind but refused to consider college after he graduated. He told me he intended to reinvent his business and this time he would make sure he did not get caught by the police.

➢ A young woman who had been sexually molested throughout her childhood and had a habit of trying to seduce her classmates, both male and female.

➢ A twenty-year-old who was arrested for concealing a gun in his wheelchair.

➢ A twenty-one- year old male who seemed only to attend so that he could sell "weed" to his classmates during class breaks. Eventually we had to dismiss him.

All these stories would seem to indicate that our classes were war zones, but they were not, even though consistent attendance was a serious problem. Within the program these young people were mostly well-mannered, grateful for a second chance, respectful to staff, open and honest with us about their problems, and ultimately very loveable and capable. That description applies to most but not all. I was never concerned for my own safety although I would admit that we had a metal detector at the entrance where we seized more than one knife. We also found knives in hidey-holes scraped out between bricks near the building entrance. Once I witnessed a shooting in our parking lot. The student was able to crawl into the building. He survived and I was traumatized.

We were able to support and teach our students well enough for 258 to graduate in ten years, forty-five in the last year alone. As a staff we were encouraged by these numbers but sad about the 750 or so that did not succeed. Twelve of our students, and even one graduate, were gunned down in the streets; the staff attended all the wakes and funerals and mourned the loss of those precious lives and tried to remain hopeful. Three more students succumbed to illness. At least one is in prison for life, without parole. But there is also the man who went on to Community College and works at a local pharmacy. And there is the young man who now works in the head office of a professional sports team but has not yet taken advantage of a college scholarship. There is the young woman who finished a CNA course and now has fulltime employment in a nursing home.

Recently I encountered a young woman at the grocery store who greeted me, saying, "I could never forget that face." We talked about her time in the GED Plus Program. Her husband was in the class too. They attended in the evening when they had someone to watch their two children. They were both very studious and determined to get their GED's. They did, quite quickly in fact. She told me that she believes that the program saved their lives. Her husband had been in some legal trouble prior to enrolling and was wanting to prove himself better than that. He has never been in trouble since that time. They are now married about 14 years and both have positions as bus monitors in the public school. Those who have never worked with young people who have slipped through the cracks in public school would never believe that this is what success in GED programs, particularly in the inner city, looks like! I am not as sure as she is that we saved their lives – they saved themselves actually – but we did provide a framework for that to happen. She made me feel more positive now about the work we did then.

The world that these students grew up in was teeming with the consequences of racism and oppression:

- Poverty. Their parents could not find a job that paid well enough for a family to survive, so families split up.

- Psychological damage. The school system was overwhelmed with the numbers of students in need of counseling.

- Prejudice. The police sometimes harassed, and some judges had no understanding of how their family circumstances and stress resulted in illegal behavior.

- Poor health care. Pediatricians in the community were overwhelmed by patients unable to pay.

- Drug abuse. Young people, from adult examples around them, believed that making a living meant selling drugs. And a sense of hopelessness sometimes led to drugs as a supposed solution.

- Gangs. Gang life made them feel as if they at least belonged somewhere. In any case, even if you were not a formal member, you were identified as a participant anyway, due to your geographical residence. One of our students, non-gang-affiliated, died in a shootout anyway just because he lived in a certain area.

- Overwhelmed caregivers. Parents would work two or three jobs and still not be able to make ends meet – and not have any family time left over. Or sometimes resorted to drugs and left the children to raise themselves.

- Constant violence.

Most of these problems are caused by a society that continues to dismiss and ignore vulnerable young people of color. Systemic racism gives the advantage to whites who then use that power to ensure that "others" do not access those same advantages equally. Young people of color are both economically and socially vulnerable. They are made to feel less-than by those who are sure they are superior. How is a young person to survive and find dignity in such an atmosphere? One cannot work with these youngsters and not see the pain and adversity that these conditions wreak, how very exposed they are. If those of us who are not actively and blatantly racist continue passively allowing such adverse conditions to continue, then we are contributing to the problem.

The behavior and lifestyles of inner-city teens should never be compared, for instance, to my own birth family and life standards. Society has not nurtured them to feel pride in their own personhood. They have not had the benefits that I had. Their urban disadvantages are in stark contrast to my own childhood circumstances in rural Maine. They do not live surrounded by the beauty of nature. Their parents do not have well-paying jobs. They did not attend drug-free high schools where students are more likely to plan dances than after-school face-offs. They did not always have enough nutritious food or maybe even food at all. Or a warm home. Peace and prosperity and learning do intersect naturally, but violence and poverty and learning are difficult to bring together and expect a positive result. My own life is not the measure by which anyone should judge those whose basic needs were unmet and opportunities, absent. We will not level the playing field between blacks and whites until we correct the results of all these years of discrimination, segregation, oppression, inequality of opportunities, condescension and racism. We need to eliminate these factors altogether if we want to realize full participation by ALL citizens, which after all can only make us a stronger nation. One observation I have made over and over through the years is that when an African American adult exhibits confidence, they probably did not grow up in Boston. What does that say about our city? Our GED Plus students were some of the most engaging, bright, personable, resilient and gifted young people I ever met. So how can we as a society dismantle the factors that keep them from their otherwise promising future of positive contributions and personal fulfillment? We would all be buoyed up by the bounty of their intelligence and creativity in full bloom.

The GED Plus work made my path an uphill one for ten years. But oh, the view from the top! What richness came into my life with every student I met! What understanding and growth came to me through every teacher and staff member! What hope I gained from the board and staff at ESAC, especially the directors! What appreciation I still feel for family and friends who understood my calling. An uphill journey yes, but not without its joys and sense of fulfillment. I was just where I was meant to be even when I witnessed that shooting. GED Plus was the best place for me to use all my experience with city children and youth, all my education – formal and informal, all my creativity, all my life experience on the bi-racial fence, and all my desire to help in reversing the effects of racism. My work was not entirely successful, but it scrambled the bricks enough to somewhat straighten the path for at least the 258 graduates. My favorite job ever, except of course being a Mom and Grandmother.

Dan's Wedding, 1998 – Bruce, Dan, Ed

"I felt that I've never seen anybody onstage talk about mixed families in a way that was positive. A lot of times interracial relationships and mixed-race kids are the brunt of the jokes on stage, so I felt like I wanted to really clear space for my family and, out of that, I really want to talk about things in the world that we can change for my daughters once they get old enough to take it over."

– W. Kamau Bell, CNN

THIRTEEN – THE KIHANYA FAMILY IN 2019

My sons had reasonably happy childhoods, I think, despite the problems. After the Ohrenberger School, Bruce and Dan both went for one year to an advanced work class and then passed the exam to be admitted to Boston Latin School, the renowned first high school in America and one of the top high schools academically in the nation. After undergoing an exam in sixth grade, those with the highest scores are admitted. Bruce was the captain of the track team there and Dan was selected as a state all-star for their league championship football team. Ed had a more difficult path in high school because of his learning challenges but was also very proud to be on the track team at Snowden International High School, from which he graduated.

Bruce went on to Boston University. Ed went to American International College after a "Thirteenth Year" at The Winchendon School. And Dan was accepted at Princeton, causing a family acquaintance (white) to say out loud that he was only admitted because he was black. Even if that were true, which it was not, Princeton would not have retained him if he could not produce in the classroom. And he graduated! This acquaintance had only one child and he dropped out of high school. The favoritism shown whites in society is likely to give you a false sense of superiority, even when there is little "better-than" in your life.

Dan, Bruce and Ed are all well-adjusted adults for many years now. They go to work every day. They go to church every week. They vote. They love and protect and care for their families. And my grandchildren are the smartest, most athletic, most beautiful two teenagers in the world!

In 1998, Dan married Molly Amble, a Michigan native of German heritage who is smart, beautiful and a superb mother. Molly does not eat dairy or gluten, but she makes delicious *stollen* for us at Christmas from an old family recipe.

In 2002, Bruce married Karen Cassar, a

native of Trinidad (Trini girl!) who is a devout Christian, with a hearty laugh and a giving spirit. Karen is mostly vegan now, along with Bruce. Even so, she makes us savory curried chicken with her own secret recipe. Both daughters-in-law are blessings to our family unit, bringing new points of view about racial differences, new knowledge of the world, and their own ideas about humanity and its foibles. I love them dearly, each and both; we are blessed that we get to embrace them as family!

My children and grandchildren identify as black but that sometimes makes for false assumptions about them, by those not fully aware of their backgrounds, both blacks and whites. Ed had an experience in high school in which a fellow African American student was pressuring him to "get down with us" and join his gang. You would have to know how gentle, well-spoken and quite formal Ed is, to predict his response: "That is not my lifestyle." Their single white Mom and their Kenyan Dad had a strong influence on our sons' character, their interests and their learning. We served them both American and Kenyan food and they all love *Ugali*, a Kikuyu dish, and also Maine lobster.

This book would not be complete without the voices of others in the family, each one of whom has a distinct and generational point of view on the topic of bi-racial families, ours in particular. These writings include interviews, stories that meander through childhood, and anecdotes that reveal who they are now. Dan and Bruce are less than a year apart so their stories from childhood overlap. Take an inside look at our 50-plus year founded family, then and now.

Dan –

In childhood I did not spend a lot of time thinking about race. There were only a few minorities in our neighborhood but ironically the neighborhood hero among the boys was a tall and powerfully built African American a few years older than me. Most of my friends were white. I don't remember many instances of white kids picking on me except at the pool where I remember a white kid pushing me under while yelling the "N" word.

During busing I was in a Roxbury inner-city school and we were bused there. Kids threw rocks at our school bus on both ends of the ride (white and black neighborhoods) because we were a mixed-race group. This was my first experience of tension between races, and with kids beyond my own neighborhood. Black kids assumed I was from their end of town and that was confusing. I did not have the knowledge they had about African American norms, Roxbury norms or really how I was supposed to act.

Boston Latin School was a still different kind of experience in that everybody there was gifted intellectually and there did not seem to be the expectation that I was this or that kind of stereotype. When I went to Princeton, the differences on campus were not about race but about class and wealth. The black students were sometimes from black economic privilege also. One close African American friend felt very isolated initially, though I did not, as I probably have a more open personality. In my dating days I dated more whites but some Asians and African Americans too. I think dating options are more open in my generation than in my parents'. One thing that still bothers me is when I go out to eat with Molly and we are made to feel conspicuous even in the more-tolerant Seattle area.

I have always felt that I should not heed any prejudice against me because of my race. I keep my head up and find a way to succeed despite people's biases. There is a problem for those of us who are bi-racial in feeling like you are not enough of any one race – you're not black enough, and certainly not white enough, to fit in solidly anywhere.

A problem for me is that society assumes that I know and love all aspects of black culture. As if I am being asked to represent the race. In my work and in terms of human resources jargon, they constantly talk about diversity, equity and inclusion. When inclusion is not present then I have found that I just have to represent myself or end up in a parade where I don't know the correct steps or rhythm!

African Americans are so very under-represented in the startup world that I work in. I never know if people are really seeing me and my experience or does their bias, conscious or otherwise, creep in? I have recently started a blog and a podcast about the lack of African Americans and Latinos in the startup world. An organization called The National Venture Capital Association did a research study in which among 2500 entrepreneurs interviewed, not even one was African American. Also, they found that less than one percent of venture capital funding goes to African American startups. One contributing factor there is that venture funders expect startups to work long hours for no pay to get started; those from impoverished circumstances cannot do that as they have no funds to fall back on.

Unfortunately, in this society, no matter what I accomplish in life, the "Nigger" dagger is always out there waiting to pierce me.

Bruce –

As a young child, I was not aware that racism even existed. I didn't think I was any different than anyone else because I was African American or had biracial parents. After a while a stranger would ask me or my mom if she was really my mom. I would feel frustrated and angry about this question. I would think, "Don't you think I know who my mom is!?"

I grew up in a neighborhood that was mostly white. There was one other black family in the area. It seemed fine to me to go play with kids that didn't look like me. A real turning point came one day at the local public pool. I was merely swimming on a hot summer day and trying to stay cool. Someone point-blank said to me, "N-----er, go back to Africa." I was shocked. Why would someone be this mean and malicious? I left the pool and walked back home in tears. I grieve over my loss of innocence that day. A child believes that the world is a wonderful, loving and trusting place to live. That day shattered any such delusion for me. Now I had to be on my guard.

At the time Hyde Park, Massachusetts, where I grew up, was not that diverse. As I look back, I suspect racism was the reason I was always assigned to right field on my little league baseball team. Even those with a casual knowledge of baseball know that very few balls are hit to right field. I suppose it also could have been that I was not as skilled as my teammates. I recall more overt expressions of racism there as well. On occasion I was called N---er from fans watching. Ironically, one of the fields where I played had been the training ground for the 54th regiment in the Civil War. This was the group of soldiers made famous in the film "Glory." They were the first African Americans to fight in the war.

I recall that my father was not intimidated at all by these situations. He came from a country that had shed its colonial master,

England, back in the 1960s. I am proud to have him as my father and he instilled in me a healthy pride, self-respect and identity.

Another turning point came when I entered the 6th grade. Up until then, I had attended a local elementary school in walking distance from my home. I was taking a school bus from Hyde Park to Roxbury to attend the Martin Luther King Jr Middle School. Again, the irony of the school name was not lost on me. It is important to understand the racial climate in Boston at the time. School busing had been implemented and it became obvious that people didn't like us travelling though their neighborhood. We were frequently pelted with rocks. It was traumatic. I don't recall that anyone ever got hurt and I am thankful for that. The emotional damage could not be avoided though.

The next year I was accepted into Boston Latin School. It was a great honor to attend this school and it still is considered the top high school in the city of Boston. I can honestly not recall many racial incidents at this school. Bad behavior was dealt with swiftly. It was a privilege to be there and an eager and well-behaved pupil was waiting in the wings to take your place if you became a disciplinary issue. I minded my business and did my schoolwork. In response to finding out that there was a black student club, a white friend asked why there was no white student club. I don't know if he was trying to make some insensitive joke or if he was really confused.

During my time at Latin School, I started running on the track team. We were part of the Dual County League. We travelled to the suburbs to compete in track meets. In my three years on the team, I saw no overt expressions of racism. I do remember witnessing an angry outburst by a runner from another team. I had just won the race and he responded by pounding his fist on the wall. I wondered if it was just simple frustration at losing, or if it was something deeper. Only God knows. I finished my time at Latin School and proudly earned my High

School diploma. I look back on that as a time of great character growth and I am grateful.

As I entered Boston University, I was hopeful that this would be a great experience. The transition was difficult for me though, as I felt lonely and homesick, even though my family was local. Many of my classmates came from mostly segregated suburban areas. Their perceptions of African Americans were clearly inaccurate, and sometimes downright offensive. I do not recall any overt expressions of racism there as it was not tolerated on the campus. The racism there was more subtle. Some students seemed to think that most black people play basketball, perform rap music and talk slang and I did none of these things. I must have seemed odd to them because I did not fit the profile they had in their minds.

As a Christian, it is inspiring to be able to worship God with those who come from many different backgrounds. It is so refreshing to see that race does not have to be a stumbling block to spiritual growth and unity in Christ. After two years at BU, I transferred to UMass Boston. This was far more diverse than what I had experienced at BU. I remember attending my first meeting of the Black Student Society. It was very enlightening to me. One of the students stood up and gave a speech that condemned racism and discrimination. I was taken aback by his intensity and the anger that poured out of him. At the time, I had moved from the dorms at BU to the Dorchester section of Boston. This was quite a transition since my new neighborhood was far more diverse than any I had lived in before.

As I got out into the working world, I came to the realization that there were not many African Americans running businesses. I had a job working at a warehouse in Roxbury. In order to deal with the tedious aspect of the workplace, a coworker brought his radio to work. This was the early 90's and it was the advent of what is known as gangster rap, music that described gritty street life without a hint of subtlety. The lyrics I heard from the radio made it clear how some musicians felt about the white race and those who had control over different aspects of society. I also realized that the N word that I heard years ago as a child was used so casually among some black folks. How could this be? This was the same word that had been used in such a derogatory manner for decades. It was the same word that had caused me emotional trauma as a child. Though I have transitioned from listening to rock and roll to rap music now, I stick to Christian rap in order to avoid the disturbing content in many of the songs. When I pull up to a red light nowadays, I sometimes hear some very offensive lyrics blaring from the car next to me, so I respond by cranking up my Christian rap.

Another issue is when some non-black folks make efforts to relate to us. I trust that in most cases this is well-meaning, but it is also misguided when they talk in slang. If someone is open to listening to me, I let them know that they should just be themselves and not try to be someone they are not.

A difficult time for me was when OJ Simpson was on trial. It seemed that everyone at my workplace wanted to know my opinion on the matter. After one or two attempts to explain how I felt, I resorted to the "no comment" response. I was the only black person at my job, so I felt like I was supposed, according to these co-workers, to be the spokesperson for the entire black race. Then when I was around black people, they expected me to side with OJ since I was black and so was he. It mattered not to most what the evidence showed. Since I did not know all the detailed evidence, I tried to avoid these conversations. I realize this is difficult terrain for those who have been the victims of discrimination and therefore, I try to show compassion to others who wish to express their own views. But I also believe that ultimate justice will be done one day as we all stand before God and give account for our lives. I recognize that this does not give comfort to those who are suffering or have lost loved ones to undeserved police brutality. There are no easy answers to these problems. I pray, as Jesus did, for unity. Will it be achieved in this lifetime?

So how would someone describe me? What expectations do they have for me? I think it is wise to simply dispense with labels and expectations and be pleasantly surprised. I am proud to be the son of multiracial parents. My very identity and makeup have given me access to richness and diversity in my life and taught me how to relate to many different groups of people. It has given me patience with those who have been wronged and need to vent their frustration. It has taught me to be tolerant of the views of others, even when they don't agree with mine. It has taught me that most of the time we can still work as a community to make this world a better place.

Now I want to speak to the boy described at the beginning of my story: "Don't be discouraged because things will get better in the city of Boston that you call home. The difficulties that threatened to derail the train of progress will serve to strengthen your character. You should play with children of all different races."

I yearn to turn back the hands of time and return to a moment before I experienced the sting of racism. The reality is that I can grieve my loss of innocence, but I cannot undo the past. I must keep moving on and help others who are willing to find a moment of clarity and see that we all need each other regardless of the color of our skin.

Ed –

My most outstanding image of bigotry from my childhood was when a substitute teacher in school pronounced my last name incorrectly. As my father had taught me, I gave him the proper pronunciation, and he said, "That sounds like a disease." He obviously did not care about my feelings. It does not sound like a disease!

In Boy Scouts I never had to deal with any kind of harassment. But you should know that I was also sometimes harassed because I was different in other ways, as a person with Asperger's Syndrome. I have had more difficulty in my life from my social deficits and learning disabilities than with racism. I had a teacher once, in tenth grade, who told my parents that I would never be able to get beyond sixth grade math, but I graduated from college!

I have always hated that black guys call each other "nigger." Even at times in school, they would call me that as a friendly gesture, but I hated it. My mother had taught me that that word was vulgar, and it is. In college, at American International College, there was a forum on race where one of the presenters explained why blacks greet each other that way. He said it is a way to identify with each other. I still do not like it.

People have often been surprised, even now, to find out who my mother is and that she's white. When she occasionally comes to my work, co-workers are surprised but never unpleasant about it. I have lived with my mother much more than I have with my father. She has been very supportive of me in my struggles with Asperger's, and thus taught me the importance of family, education and a love for people who are different from me. As she shared her faith with me, I learned about compassion for others, especially the less fortunate, generosity, and a desire for justice. She always made sure that we were aware of racial issues and I have pursued that interest right up until now. One thing that she always emphasized is that we should treat women with respect.

My father had a lot of influence on me too, naturally, as a father does, but also as a role model. He taught me the importance of self-discipline and personified that for me in his own life. He also emphasized the importance of my Christian faith and how I should pray and read the Bible regularly and stand up for my beliefs.

He wanted me to know and understand my Kenyan roots, particularly Kikuyu. He encouraged me to read Facing Mt. Kenya in order to know about the birth of Kenyan and

Kikuyu culture. Whenever I have done something significant or important in my life, he has reminded me that I am a Kihanya, a proud name and that I represent our family. He told me all about my relatives in Kenya, although I have never met them. He taught me the meaning of the name Kihanya (good shepherd).

He talked to me about Kenya's fight for independence from the British as a way to encourage me to be strong in the face of difficult situations. He also told me that because he didn't want me to think of myself as less than anyone else because of my race and ethnicity. He never wanted me to let my racial or ethnic background become an obstacle to showing people what I have to offer the world. My father taught me to be a man, to be strong but also compassionate. He said I should not be afraid to ask for help when I need it.

My dad especially liked to tell us stories about climbing Mount Kilimanjaro and tales from his years at Alliance High School. He speaks fondly of learning to cook as he watched his mother in the kitchen. He taught me about education, always to take it seriously and value it, but never to think of myself as limited in terms of what I could accomplish. Regarding my learning disability, he was hyper-vigilant about how I was treated by teachers and he always said that I could overcome my challenges. Looking back, I think that helped me and gave me the determination to do that because I thought so too.

Molly –

My kids were born when I was living in the Boston area. When my youngest was born many people asked me where she was from. I was very tempted to say, "my WOMB" several times but mostly the folks asking were kind Asian women who were trying to make conversation. Then I moved back to the San Francisco area, and I'll never forget the first time I went to Trader Joe's with my two kids. There were at least three other white moms with brown children in the store

– I'd found my place. One time at Berkeley Bowl (natural food co-op), when I was standing in line for fish, a beautiful African woman looked at my daughter, about 3 years old, and said how beautiful she was. As she looked closer, she noted that my daughter had beautiful African lips and mouth. I can't tell you how happy that made me feel!

In my biased opinion – my kids are gorgeous. When they were infants/toddlers Benetton and The Gap were using mixed race children in all of their ads. One time outside of Boston, when my kids were about 4 and 6 years old, we were at a pumpkin farm on a hayride and another man in the wagon started taking pictures of them. I blocked the photos, subtly at first, then I asked him what he was doing. He said he was a photographer from a local paper. I don't recall if he got any photos at that time but from THAT MOMENT on, I never let my kids be photographed. I was the mom who DIDN'T sign the form for their kids' photos to be on advertising for school or whatever activity. I had worked in school admissions and I knew how every photo has to have a mix of diverse people, and if my kids were photographed, I knew they would be the ones chosen. One summer, my daughter was about 11 years old and participated in the Vacation Bible School at church. I never saw a consent form but was surprised when a well-meaning and excited mom said, "Did you see your daughter's photo on the front page of the local newspaper?" While I wasn't happy, it was proof of my theory. Now the kids are older, and they can choose if they want their photos taken. They could probably both be models – and yes, I'm biased.

Lily –

I am sixteen years old and live in a suburb of Seattle. I feel good about being bi-racial. At many times it is a blessing. I see various perspectives of both Caucasian and African American cultures. I believe that it has con-tributed to my open-mindedness about others' opinions. I am intrigued by foreign and indigenous cultures and languages. Through my strength of observation and awareness, I know that not all people are as respectful and interested in unknown ways of living and speaking as I am. I believe that to stem from white privilege, something extremely prevalent in the city I live in. White privilege exists without a doubt. It is an issue that must be tackled first through awareness of its presence in one's daily life. Regularly, I notice students taking for granted having two parents in the same household, applying for colleges, driving their own car, or having a free computer for schoolwork. I catch myself taking these matters for granted even though they are not so simple for others. I am very blessed to be in a financially stable family, but I am aware of a lack of commonality in that aspect.

Although I see both races, the good and the bad of each, I find it difficult to reso-nate with so-called "black culture" as I did not grow up in a predominately black community. Stereotypes of black culture are too common and perhaps very dangerous.

The topic of my race, or shall I say races, is not a hot topic for me. People generally assume that I am black. White and black. What does that really mean? Do I know? Do they know? Why is there a hard line between being white and being black? I struggle finding my place because of this hard line in society. I struggle with these philosophical questions. It is usually a shock when I tell people that I am only ¼ African. I notice now while writing this piece that I have become accustomed to describing my African heritage as "only" this amount. Subconsciously I see the pattern of people assuming my heritage to be mostly or all African American. This issue of the phrases "white" and "black" to describe race seems only relevant when referring to Caucasian or African people. This excludes far too many races, which is another issue.

My Asian bi-racial friends do not experience assumptions about their race. I am sure they face other problems regarding their race but from my observation, they are exempt from this one. For my Korean/

Caucasian, or Indian/Caucasian friends, no one assumes anything about them. They are either thought to be only "white" or "Asian," not somewhere in between like me. Of course, this is generalizing for the sole purpose of analyzing racial issues within my own two races.

One majority in my city is Asian. The large Asian community is overwhelming for me. It is so tight knit that I feel as though I am missing out on meeting new people and going to social events because I do not have connection within that community. Some of my Asian friends and their families are engrossed in their own community. At times, I feel excluded and almost frustrated that they are not aware of the unintentional exclusion this creates.

I feel uncomfortable when the tough topics of race and minorities are discussed. It is that feeling of everyone's eyes on you. I feel almost obliged to share my opinion to represent the minority of African Americans in my school and community. This puts so much unnecessary pressure on me that I try to let it go.

To close, I want to share a benefit I experienced from voicing my thoughts. During a session of social and emotional learning at my school I shared the discomfort and discontent one experiences when another person touches his/her hair without permission. It is the most flattering and yet intolerable encounter. My lovely teacher emailed later about how much she valued my perspective and insightful comment. She shared her awareness of me being a minority in my school. I was elated reading it because this might be the first written confirmation that I have of anyone in my school being aware of the African American minority in my school. Finally, I knew for sure that at least one other person, besides my brother, is aware of this minority group because I have it in writing to look back on forever. This gave me hope that more people in my community can gain awareness about this issue of diversity across our city.

Michael –

Being bi-racial has taught me to have patience when people are quick to judge me just on my looks rather than who I am inside. It also has made me more aware of many cultures than most of my friends. There have also been people over the years who have tried to make me feel bad about myself. The sport I like to play most is lacrosse and there are not many black kids who do. Sometimes someone from the crowd of another school will make a comment like: "Why are you playing this game when lacrosse is for white kids?" After all, the inventors of lacrosse were people of color, Native Americans. It's rare but a few people have called me the "N" word. I try to ignore it and just keep playing.

Usually as a friendly gesture kids will ask me "What's your makeup?" and I am happy to tell them. I see myself as someone who cares about family, school, lacrosse and my friends. I really like to have fun! Though I am light-skinned, I have never been in a position where someone thought I was white. They seem to already have me in the African American category, maybe because of my hair. Up until now I have mostly preferred to wear my hair long because I like it that way. As far as I know my racial makeup has not been a factor in who my friends are or who I would want to date. It is more important to me how they make me feel.

I mostly grew up in a white culture because my mom and three of my four grandparents have been white. I have also enjoyed spending time with my Grandpa Kihanya. I think I would like to be that kind of grandfather – one who has made us laugh and is just the best storyteller. I am named after him (middle name) so he and Kenya are both very important to me. I admire his perseverance in all that he has overcome.

My African American heroes are jazz musician Miles Davis, rapper Kendrick Lamar, Dr. Martin Luther King, football player Randy Moss, director Jordan Peele, and President Obama.

Kathy –

For those who were once worried about how my bi-racial family would evolve over generations, the writings above give a great indication of how both our social and physical traits are developing. My own heritage: short stature, long torsos, curly hair, baldness, allergies, and diabetes from the Phillips (maternal) side. Long legs, prominent noses, some strain of Autism/Asperger's, a tendency to anger, Methodism and blond hair/blue eyes from the Grannells (paternal.) From both – above average intelligence, Christian belief, life spans that do not exceed eighty years and poor vision. And for the 1905-1988 season that we resided in Rumford, Maine, home also to a paper mill, an extremely high rate of cancer due to water and air pollution in our childhoods. Four of the five children of my parents have had cancer, as did my mother. And yes, a pink/white tone of the epidermis and a limited interaction with people of color, until 1966.

David's heritage from the hills of Kenya: short stature, curly hair, above average intelligence, respect for education, Christian belief, life without technology (at that time), delicious food, oppression and victimization, allergies, survival instincts, physical strength, longevity, and brown eyes. And a deep bronze pigment of the epidermis. And Kikuyu and Swahili and English languages.

What will that heritage look like as it transitions to our grandchildren and beyond? For one thing there are increasing numbers of bi-racial and multi-racial people in the United States. One would hope that the increasing mix would reduce oppression as time goes by.

All of the above will be inherited by my grandchildren as they grow into their own selves. Lily has the long legs of her maternal grandmother. Michael has eyebrows that probably came from my line. They both have my math ability and David's interest in science and technology. They have brown hair with a few reddish highlights in summer, and light-bronze skin which also deepens in summer. Michael has allergies and Lily has a beautiful singing voice all her own. Both are great athletes like Dan and Molly. They are both fluent in French and spiritual, highly intelligent, kind, and a compilation of everything Kihanya-Kariuki-Amble-Duell-Grannell-Phillips. Lily is a perfectionist and Michael not so much. No long noses, no short legs, no bad teeth or poor vision. A mixture of the nature and nurture of the generations before them, just like everybody else!!

Fourth of July on Chebeague, 2004 –
Michael Kihanya, Kiana Sawyer, Anna Whitaker

"If anything, I think the day will come when people won't look at where people come from, the history of their culture, of the race. I think the day will come when we'll see people as human beings and not someone who's a son or daughter of the formerly enslaved, as someone from Africa or of African heritage or Irish or Italian and we'll just be citizens of America and citizens of the world. And we will forget about origin and color and race."

   – John Lewis, Representative from Georgia

FOURTEEN – UP 'TIL NOW:
THUS FAR ON THE WAY

In the book, <u>Waking Up White</u>, by Debby Irving, she provides a list of "white culture behaviors" that uphold our whites-first society. On it are such items as conflict avoidance, valuing formal education over life experience, entitlement, competitiveness, and belief in only one right way. As I look at the list now, I see that until I met David, I was adhering to those behaviors one hundred percent. Maybe, and just maybe, I have veered from that straight road about fifty percent – and that took fifty-three years. This is definitely a lifelong journey, and then on to the next generation to make further progress. I see the errors of my ways and yet I have not been able to just turn them off. I still catch myself feeling entitled sometimes. My grandmother's adages are still deep within me – "Don't make a fuss!" I have even tried giving up being judgmental for Lent. That worked. A little. I can only keep on listening, learning, trying and caring.

So how does a white person like me fit in? How should I fit in? For the truth is, I do not seem to fit in at all, though better than I did fifty years ago. One dear African American friend has in the past made jokes about my being "black" myself, because of my African American family and because of my still-nascent understanding of racism, I suppose. I used to think that was funny too and took secret pride in her gesture of acceptance. Then came the case of Rachel Dolezal-Diallo (with the legal name, Nkechi Amare Diallo). She was living as an African American. Her parents came forth to announce that Rachel is actually, biologically, white. Before that time, she was an instructor of African studies at Eastern Washington University and President of the Spokane, Washington, NAACP. After the news of her deception was broadcast, she was immediately dismissed from both positions.

Ms. Dolezal-Diallo still claims to be "trans-racial." That of course is a new word and borrowed from the concept of trans-gender in which there are permanent biological and hormonal changes undertaken. In the case of Ms. Dolezal there is no vital necessity for changing her racial identity, only her desire to do so. And her attempts to look like a black person were only temporary and cosmetic. For me, the idea of "trans-racial" is a temporary denial of self and therefore misguided and distressing and detrimental to people on both sides of the color line.

There was also the case of author John Howard Griffin who in the 1960's made his skin black in order to document the treatment of African-Americans in the south at that time, and to discover how that treatment was different from his usual experience as a white person. That research, recorded in his book, <u>Black Like Me</u>, at least benefitted society through education. It was temporary and meaningful. It gave us insights into the treatment of blacks and the resulting everyday feelings of blacks. For instance, the author wrote, "Once again a 'hate stare' drew my attention like a magnet. It came from a middle-aged, heavy-set, well-dressed white man. He sat a few yards away, fixing his eyes on me. Nothing can describe the withering horror of this. You feel lost, sick at heart before such unmasked hatred, not so much because it threatens you as because it shows humans in such an inhuman light. You see a kind of insanity, something so obscene the very obscenity of it (rather than its threat) terrifies you." Without a rationale that benefits everyone and with no revelation of truth, cultural appropriation is wrong, whether it is from white to black or black to white.

That Dolezal-Diallo incident made me consider once again who I am within the multiracial and racial landscape. I would never appropriate a race or culture not my own, as Ms. Dolezal-Diallo did. By skin tone and status, I am white. I am more prone to skin cancer; I am more likely to be hired and I am less likely to be imprisoned for minor crimes. I am now equally at ease with white and black members of society, but I did not earn the privilege of being called "Black," nor is that possible. I have not fully endured racism; I *could* still walk away into a mostly white world and not look back. I never would but I could; I have a choice. I did not celebrate the successes and struggles of black folks as I myself experienced them, but rather as a bystander and ally. I voted for Obama but thought OJ guilty.

My ancestors were not oppressed, and some may have even been complicit in the oppression, it pains me to say. I cannot even apologize for them and they are not here to do that themselves. My ancestral history was not cut off in the middle by slavery; that factor has virtually disabled all systems of keeping track of ancestry for African Americans. Any attempts by black folks, even now, to trace their ancestry means rebuilding the possible family tree and starting over, often with DNA tracing. My forebears were never forced to live away from their spouses and children, or forbidden to read and write, another difficulty in passing down knowledge of lineage to next generations. African American is a regal title, combining strength and resilience with racial pride. I have not earned that title any more than Ms. Dolezal did, and I do not deserve it. My whiteness excludes me from that category even if my children and grandchildren can claim it. I do love though when a Latina friend calls me, "Blanca." We laugh about that, but it is true!

For a long time, the inaccuracy of naming all black people African Americans has been a concern for me; my children are second generation African Americans. So why is it, within such terminology, that we lump all African countries together as if they were all one country? Likely because many African Americans cannot pinpoint which country their ancestors were kidnapped into slavery from – without a DNA test. My sons are actually Kenyan-American. On the other hand, folks whose ancestors came directly into slavery in the United States have a different family heritage than those who were brought to the West Indies before ultimately arriving here. And even African Americans whose families escaped slavery and went to the North earlier than others have a heritage that stands in contrast to families that remained enslaved for generations. And Africans who emigrated here and are now first- or second-generation Americans, like David Kihanya, have an even more distinct heritage from the others. So even within the diaspora there are differences in heritage and gradations in their history of being oppressed. And yet we seem to label them all "black" or "African American."

During the last few years, racism has become more blatant once again in our nation. For most of my adult life it was kept on the down low. Folks had gradually begun to be at least civil and cut back on name-calling, but it was still simmering just beneath the surface of course. The election of President Obama became a rallying point for some to say, "Now they've gone too far and need to be put back in their place," and to claim that this a "post-racial" America.

The recent protest over the picture of a bi-racial child on the cover of Cheerios boxes was initially dispiriting to me. Racists claimed that this was an encouragement for those who want to blur race lines with bi-racial children. Ultimately, I became encouraged and elated when, in what I saw as counter-offensive, there was suddenly a marked increase in bi-racial and multi-racial ads on television. White dads with bi-racial daughters and even one ad with a black woman trying out a mattress with (supposedly) her white husband (or partner). Now there is even a shampoo product line for bi-racial folks named, "Mixed Chicks." I learned this from my granddaughter! One step back on the path, two steps forward! It feels good when you and yours are represented in the media!

Lately I consider how it is that one can combat racism, try to lessen its effect on my family and still be my white self, all at the same time? It is not an easy road, but it must be traveled by multi-racial families – all families really – in order to find self-confidence and self-worth for all involved. It is a day-by-day process. You make mistakes. You fall and get back up. You seek solid friendships from many cultures that help you progress. You hurt people's feelings unwittingly, and then you LISTEN. And when someone tells you that you just committed a racial or ethnic gaffe, you apologize and ensure that you never do it again because those slighted in such situations are the experts on what is racist. You study the history of other folks just as much as you study your own. You seek out movies and books that give insight into a particular culture. You read biographies of its cultural and historical leaders. You eat food that you never have before. You encourage your children to espouse both of their inherited cultures and, more importantly, their unique identity as bi-racial and multicultural persons. You hold your own head high and struggle through. And you pray. And engage in uneasy conversations and **listen**. A lot. Even though I am an avid reader, I have learned much more through person-to-person experience.

When you have a physical pain, an excruciating one that will just not go away, you do anything you can to ease it and to get rid of it altogether. Aspirin, Tylenol. Heat, ice. Call the hotline nurse. Visit the emergency room. Call your primary care doctor. Have x-rays, MRI, CAT scans. Go to physical therapy. Take pain pills. Have a cortisone shot. Whatever it takes to get rid of the pain. Racism is an excruciating pain in our nation. On a scale of one-to-ten, it is beyond ten. It is a pain that has just not gone away. We have passed laws that have eased it a bit, but not cured it. We have had leaders who have fought for equality and justice and told us what we need to do to eliminate it. Yet it still aches incessantly. We have analyzed it and produced data that prove it still exists. We have protested in the streets, honored our Civil Rights leaders and formed committee after committee, task force after task force and yet. Racism is. Right now, blatantly so. Sometimes undercover. Sometimes overtly. Black folks, particularly men, are disproportionately and unfairly treated in the justice system. Young people are killed in the streets to the tune of "Take that, you N---" Inner-city children receive insufficient educations and drink filthy water and go without adequate food and health care. We should do no less than combat, dismantle and unpack the racism, not just alleviate it here and there, but eliminate it altogether. Get rid of the pain. GET RID OF THE PAIN!

I am discouraged by statistics that delineate a steadily growing academic racial achievement gap, and hunger, economic and healthcare gaps, all of which are inter-related in many ways. All the indicators of upward mobility in American society show people of color lagging behind. At this very moment (February 2019) there are 14,600 children confined near our border with Mexico – all children of color. The African American unemployment and incarceration rates are unfairly much higher than those for whites. At the same time, there seems to be increasing awareness of, and action to eliminate the "school-to-prison pipeline," as defined by research and data. This work enhances the possibility of a cure for the circumstances causing the pipeline in the first place. Unfortunately, it is likely to be very gradual.

Regrets are those things that did not happen in your life, though you wish now that they had. Maya Angelou once said, "Forgive yourself for not knowing what you didn't know before you learned it." So, regrets are what you might personally have done and cannot go back and rectify now, even if you wanted to. I have no regret that I married David, even though it ended in divorce. By virtue of that union I have lived a much richer and more interesting life than I would have otherwise. Not to mention that I cannot envision a life without my dear sons, their wonderful wives or my stellar grandchildren.

The problem in my marriage was never race, and that was obvious to me from the beginning. It was culture that made our differences irreparable. Dictionary.com defines culture as "the customs, arts, social institutions, and achievements of a particular nation, people, or other social group, and the attitudes and behavior characteristic of a particular social group." It affects daily interactions and communication. It is ingrained from childhood and almost impossible to expunge or even change, even if the individual is willing. It affects personal habits, home décor, views on education and religion, nutrition, and health care – and on and on. Food, clothing and holidays are the least of the differences – those are more easily swapped off. One example for us is that when Dan was born, David wanted to buy a whole goat, bring it to our apartment kitchen, cut it up and then roast it. To begin with, we did not have the implements and pans necessary. And from there, what would the landlord think? And yet without that rite, David was saddened.

David and I have continued to communicate about family matters through now twenty-five years of divorce and forty years total of legal separation. When I married him, I also espoused all that he was and all that society perceived him to be. On the fiftieth anniversary of our marriage, September 17, 2016, I took note of the fifty years, and telephoned David just to acknowledge that history. Neither of us has married again.

But still, **regrets**. I have a few. Maybe more than a few, in no particular order:

- I have had too many overly emotional reactions to racist events, and thus forfeited teachable moments, for me and for others.

- I did not provide my sons with as much interaction with black folks as I should have in their childhood. The neighborhood was not very diverse.

- Our divorce allowed those opposed to our marriage to say, "I told you so!"

- The type of professional work I engaged in was not very profitable. It is confusing in that I do not regret the work itself.

- I have never been to Kenya, nor have Bruce and Ed.

- At various times in youth I wanted to be a

secretary like my mother, or a librarian or to be a minister in the church. I never achieved any of those. Not sure this is a regret though.

- I did not wear a white dress for our wedding, for the practical reason that it should be something I could wear again. The plum-colored suit I see in the pictures does not seem celebratory at all.

In my hometown there is a cable suspension footbridge that was constructed in 1931 by the paper mill company, to facilitate workers' access to the mill. At that time not many workers had automobiles and my family was no exception. The bridge spans the Androscoggin River between the most populated section of town and the mill itself. It is probably 300 feet end-to-end. Further upstream is the base of Rumford Falls, which we were taught to claim is "the biggest falls east of Niagara." Water thunders and rages down that falls for about one-half mile, under the two bridges for automobiles, around a slight bend, and right beneath that footbridge — about <u>200 feet</u> down! Though very convenient for those like my Dad who walked over it to get to their day or night shifts, it was very hazardous, with see-through railings, and children were regularly warned of its grave danger. Before we owned a car, my Dad would occasionally take me with him over the footbridge, to get his paycheck. In addition to the river making a powerful, angry whoosh!! Right there, the bridge itself literally swung side-to-side with each footstep. Very, very terrifying for a little girl! I remember one time when I was so scared that I asked, "Daddy, please, please let's go back." He picked me up and told me that it would make no sense to go back when we were closer to the other end of the bridge, so we continued on.

My adult life has been much like that — threatening sometimes, feeling carried sometimes, but always, always, looking for the end of the bridge. After my first footstep on the swinging bridge that became my life after September 1966, there was no turning back. I was already more than halfway across the color line but, unlike the footbridge, I would never make it to the other side. I have been in that never-never-land between white life and black life, still swinging back and forth. Perhaps my life, and the life of those in my family, can serve as some measure of a bridge between a divided and a united racial world. That, at least, would give our lives more meaning. My humble wish is that we all stop excluding, defining, limiting, and degrading each other and instead accept and celebrate who each of us is – and seek to understand each other so that the bridge stops swinging

So: still free? Probably. Still white – sure, with lots of age spots, and many emotional scars from the fray of bi-racial parenting. Still twenty-one? No. A much wiser and much more racially conscious seventy-three. As my mother would say, "Old enough to know better." And now to see how my grandchildren fare out there in the world. Have the atmosphere, the laws and society changed in fifty years? Probably, but not always for the better, and definitely not enough. At least Michael and Lily can legally marry whomever they want when the time comes.

I used to be afraid to get bored, but that never happened. Now I welcome the peace and quiet and time to explore where I have been, how things have changed and where my family and the world are going from here. Herein I have traced my path from Rumford to Tufts to Hyde Park to Roxbury to Milton. And from a pale white life to a diverse, inclusive and better one. I have learned from each step along the way. I no longer expect to make as much of a difference, but rather I want to analyze if I ever did. Maybe I made some tiny progress toward my dream of a better world for my children and grandchildren. I expect they will make a bigger difference. I never wanted to do anything but be an example of what could be. I hope at least that I have done that. When I see young inter-racial families now it warms my soul.

My journey is no longer along a path or a

road but rather now a highway, zooming into a future where perhaps the human race will sometime be a mixed race – or maybe not. The road behind me is now much longer than the road ahead. I expect delays, for I am sure there are still some speedbumps and potholes ahead. And construction. But still I journey on, for I am only "thus far on the way."

"I leave you love.
I leave you hope.
I leave you the challenge of developing confidence in one another.
I leave you a thirst for education.
I leave you a respect for the use of power.
I leave you faith. I leave you racial dignity.
I leave you a desire to live harmoniously with your fellow men.
I leave you finally, a responsibility to our young people."

- Mary McLeod Bethune

Chebeague Island, 2012 -All Kihanyas:
David, Ed, Michael, Karen, Lily, Kathy, Bruce, Molly, Dan

"We the people of the United States are amazingly rich in elements from which we weave a culture. We have the best of man's past on which to draw, brought to us by our native folk and folk from all parts of the world. In binding these elements into a national fabric of beauty and strength, let us keep the original fibers so intact that the fineness of each will show in the completed handiwork."

– President Franklin D. Roosevelt

EPILOGUE

In fifty-three years, some things that have changed little:

- Some police are still accosting white and multiracial people for no good reason, sometimes with dire consequences.

- Massachusetts' Racial Imbalance Act of 1965 is still in effect and governs the population mix and how it is distributed among schools in all towns and cities of the Commonwealth. It ensures that we will not go back to segregated schools.

- The Kihanyas still spend our summer vacations in Maine after 43 years.

- The bus route from Roslindale Square to Dudley station is now part of a longer route and is still running after 30 years.

- The GED Plus Program at ESAC (now known as the ESAC Youth Opportunity Youth Collaborative) continues to encourage school dropouts to implement their scholastic and professional dreams.

- My grandson is in the process of applying to colleges right now. One of the items on his wish list is that the college have diversity in its student population.

Some things that have changed more:

- The rate of interracial weddings in the United States has increased to 17% in 2017, up from 3% in 1966. (Pew Research Center)

- My grandchildren are growing up on the west coast where biracial families, all kinds of combinations, are very common.

- Interracial and interethnic married couples grew by 28 percent over the decade. – 2010 U.S. Census

- Loving Day, June 12, the anniversary of the Supreme Court *Loving v. Virginia* decision, is now celebrated by multiracial families around the nation.

- The number of mixed-race Americans is increasing three times faster than the population of the United States as a whole. In the 1970s, one percent of American children were of mixed race. Now, 10 percent are. (Pew Research Center)

- Rumford's population has declined by half since the mid-1960's. However, the African American population has risen from near zero to 1.4%. The nearby city of Lewiston now has a black population of 4.3%, mostly due to an influx of Somali refugees, but the process for integrating the immigrants there has not been smooth. (U.S. Census) No one growing up there now will be able to say that they have never seen a black person.

- Martin Luther King Day is a federal holiday now and celebrated in every state.

- The Boston Public Schools is presently spending more time and resources on lowering the racial achievement gap than they are on busing.

- The United Methodist Church is grappling with a new diversity, that of LBGTQ congregants, pastors and marriages. It is very possible that the church will split into two camps over this issue. Another frontier to cross.

- Both Catholic schools that I worked in, St. Andrew and St. Joseph, are now closed.

- David now suffers with a significant loss of memory and lives in an assisted living facility. His sons are devoted to him and his care. I am proud of them for that. I always wanted them to stay connected to their father. Fathers are especially important for bi-racial sons.

- I journey on with the aid of a cane.

How **I am different**:

1. I understand the life and legacy of Malcolm X much better now, and also the peaceful protest of Muhammad Ali which gives me insight into the actions of Colin Kaepernick.

2. I think often about the racial and political assassinations that dominated the 1960's and wonder what might have been if those four men had lived on.

3. In 2003 I visited all through England, Ireland, Scotland and Wales with my sister Jan. That trip enlightened me

about the roots of whites feeling superior, and how it is not always a positive thing to claim British heritage,

4. I still check the BPD News (police) report every day, praying that I will not see a name I know from GED Plus.

5. I try not to think of either my birth family or my founded family as the standard for others anymore. And I listen when others accuse me of that.

6. I still seek out diversity in friendships; my friends now embody an amazing variety of ethnicities, cultures, native lands and race(s). But I never say, "Some of my best friends…"

7. I look forward to all the new cultures that will come into our extended family through marriage in the years to come.

8. I have plenty of time now to look back and appreciate all the blessings of my life. God has blessed me mightily.

The stories that I have presented here were collected day-by-day in an otherwise "normal" life. However, the collective reality that they construct could make our Kihanya lives a prototype for bi-racial families. Maybe.

9. "Two roads diverged in a wood, and I—
   I took the one less traveled by,
   And that has made all the difference."
   ~ Robert Frost

TIMELINE

1940– David Kariuki Kihanya born in Nakuru, Kenya

1945– Kathryn Isabel Grannell born in Rumford, Maine, U.S.A.

1963– Kathy enters Tufts University, Medford, MA

1965– David Kihanya becomes an exchange student at Tufts University

1966– Marriage of David and Kathryn, Bedford, MA

1967– Birth of Daniel Kariuki Kihanya, Boston, MA

1967- Birth of Bruce Grannell Kihanya, Boston, MA

1972– Birth of Edward Muruthi Kihanya, Boston, MA

1974– Start of court-ordered busing in Boston

1975– George Grannell becomes the sole owner of the family homestead on Chebeague Island, Maine

1978-87– Kathy works as Multicultural Coordinator in Boston Public Schools

1979 – Legal separation of David and Kathryn

1988– Project A.C.T.S. bus action in Roslindale

1988-90– Kathryn earns a master's degree in Education at Curry College

1990-92– Kathy teaching at St. Andrew School, Jamaica Plain, MA

1992-99– Kathy is teacher and administrator at St. Joseph School, Roxbury, MA

1994– Divorce of David and Kathryn

1998- Marriage of Dan and Molly

2000 – Birth of Michael David Kihanya

2001-2011 – Kathy becomes director of GED Plus, Roxbury, MA

2002 – Marriage of Bruce and Karen

2003 – Birth of Lillian Amble Kihanya

2011 – Kathy retires

2017 – David enters assisted living.

ABOUT THE AUTHOR

Kathryn Isabel Grannell was born in 1945 in Rumford, Maine.

She attended Rumford schools, graduating from Stephens High School in 1963. She then entered Jackson College at Tufts University, receiving a Bachelor of Arts degree, having majored in French and Education. She also studied reading education at Curry College, receiving a Master of Education in 1990.

Beyond her family and community, Kathryn dedicated 30 plus years to a career in education throughout Boston.

Kathryn was married to David Kihanya in 1966. She is very proud of her three sons – Daniel, Bruce and Edward, her two daughters-in-law Molly and Karen and her two grandchildren – Michael and Lily.

Kathryn resides in Milton, Massachusetts.

Made in the USA
Columbia, SC
28 November 2019